BELINDA TERRO MOONEY WITH GIANNA T. MOONEY

My Therapeutic Lifestyle Changes Workbook

First published by Belinda Terro Mooney 2021

Copyright © 2021 by Belinda Terro Mooney with Gianna T. Mooney

All rights reserved. No part of this publication may be reproduced, stored or transmitted in any form or by any means, electronic, mechanical, photocopying, recording, scanning, or otherwise without written permission from the publisher. It is illegal to copy this book, post it to a website, or distribute it by any other means without permission.

First edition

ISBN: 978-1-955225-02-1

This book was professionally typeset on Reedsy.
Find out more at reedsy.com

This workbook is dedicated to my children and my students at Lone Star College Montgomery Campus. You are a blessing in my life, and it has been my privilege to teach all of you.

If I can stop one heart from breaking,
I shall not live in vain;
If I can ease one life the aching,
Or cool one pain,
Or help one fainting robin
Unto his nest again,
I shall not live in vain.

                         – Emily Dickinson

Contents

Acknowledgement	ii
Disclaimer	iii
Praise for "My Therapeutic Lifestyle Changes Workbook"	iv
Introduction	viii
1 Therapeutic Lifestyle Changes	1
2 Identifying Current Status, Goals, Strengths, and Resources	16
3 Writing TLCs: Typical First Try, Better, and Best Versions	33
4 Creating Your TLCs	49
5 Implementing Your TLCs with Accountability	68
6 Beginning Again	71
Strengths	73
Resources (Support from Outside Yourself)	76
Daily Checklist of TLCs	77
Glossary	78
Bibliography and Extra Reading	80
What Do You Think?	88
About the Author	89

Acknowledgement

A big thank you to all my students in many classes, who used the original template and "field tested" the workbook (especially Amy, Courtney, Deena, Leonard, Tina, and Vanessa). Also, thank you to all my colleagues, (especially Terry Albores, Leanne Crowe, Scott Hankosky, Allen Ivey, Glen Killian, and Cynthia Trumbo), and my friends (especially Rebecca Mentzer), who used and reviewed this workbook and gave me input and many suggestions for improving it. Thanks to my daughter Gianna (who helped me keep writing when tragedy came) and my son Justin (who did the lion's share of the work in our home so I could write), who gave me the courage to finish.

Disclaimer

This workbook is not meant to provide medical, nutritional, or therapeutic advice but simply to encourage you to pursue good health by creating the habits and the lifestyle that will allow you to maintain recovery and health. Consult your doctor or another professional (for instance, a nutritionist or therapist) and your sponsor to get input on whether your goals are reasonable or would harm you in any way. This workbook is not meant to replace professional advice but to just help you get started.

Praise for "My Therapeutic Lifestyle Changes Workbook"

"No matter what your line of work, *My Therapeutic Lifestyle Changes Workbook* will help you live life in a more holistic and healthy manner. While we all ask the inevitable questions, 'What am I here for? . . . What is the meaning of life?' the answers do not fully reveal all the details of how to live while we are here. Trying to circumnavigate the world without a compass and a map is probably not the wisest decision. What *My Therapeutic Lifestyle Changes Workbook* does is provide the reader with what one might call 'life's navigational help,' whether you are simply seeking a better night's sleep or facing more challenging matters such as combatting addiction, avoiding burnout, or repairing a dysfunctional relationship.

It's all well and good to know your purpose in life—but exactly how best do you reduce your stress, focus your energy, simplify your decisions, and give the fullest meaning to your life and the lives of others? This workbook introduces a therapeutic paradigm that provides you with many tools for the journey we call life, whether you're married or single, whether you're an accountant, computer programmer, or therapist in need of your own rejuvenation."

—Professor Michael A. Brinda, author of *Parish Management and Operations: The Buck Stops Here*

"*My Therapeutic Lifestyle Changes Workbook* is a wonderful tool for helping professionals, regardless of whether they're just entering the field or a 'seasoned veteran.' Thorough, insightful, and practical, it's a must-have for yourself and your clients!"

—Glen Killian, MA, LPC, Professor of Human Services, Director, Human

Services Program, Lone Star College Montgomery

"*My Therapeutic Lifestyle Changes Workbook* utilizes effective methods to help anyone make positive changes and work toward specific goals with accountability. These changes can lead to a balanced lifestyle and prevent burnout. I highly recommend *My Therapeutic Lifestyle Changes Workbook.*"

—Leanne Crowe, MS (marriage, family, child counseling) Adjunct Professor of Human Services, Lone Star College Montgomery

"I first used the [TLC workbook format] as a student in Professor Mooney's class. Using the TLCs has helped me in many areas of my life, such as with stress management, exercise, and educational goals. Using the TLCs helped me know where to focus and move toward my goals with ease and lasting changes in my life. I have been waiting for months for *My Therapeutic Lifestyle Changes Workbook* to be released so I can introduce my clients to the TLCs and watch them make lasting change in their lives. Anyone who uses TLCs will see remarkable improvement in their lives!"

—Tina M. Torres LCDC-I, Senior-Level Social Work Student

"I have never been one to journal. Then I took a basic counseling class with Professor Belinda Terro Mooney. We had an assignment to complete a workbook. My first thought was 'Oh no, a journal!' This workbook was uniquely designed to have you look at your life as it is, where it needs to go, how to get there, and why. This workbook exposed me to some things that I didn't know I could do or needed to do. I was on an emotional roller coaster while doing this project. I cried, laughed, dreamed, got upset, and found peace during the journey. I now have wellness goals, spiritual goals, financial goals, and life and career goals that I am consciously working toward. I can truly say that this workbook has changed my lifestyle for the best."

—Deena B., Basic Counseling Skills Student

"*My Therapeutic Lifestyle Changes Workbook* is an accessible and practical resource to support flourishing with a clear roadmap and action steps. I recommend using this resource in pursuing holistic wellness in an achievable way!"

—Rebecca Mentzer, B.S. Economics

"I love the chapter on encouraging people to make healthy lifestyle changes. Belinda Terro Mooney will help you focus on key issues concerning health promotion for individuals in this new therapeutic lifestyle workbook."

—Scott Hankosky, MS, Wellness Instructor, Lone Star College

"My Therapeutic Lifestyle Changes Workbook is a powerful and highly accessible resource to help everyone, especially those with addictions or those suffering trauma, lead a calmer, more balanced and well-ordered life. Belinda Terro Mooney provides readers with the necessary tools to create good habits, and the workbook format aids in implementing and sustaining these changes. I believe this book will be the answer to prayer for many people."

— Karen Barbieri, founder of Pietra Fitness

"This workbook is one of the best ones I have ever come across. It has helped me to evaluate and re-evaluate my life. It gave me the opportunity to make a weekly schedule which helped myself with finding that special 'me' time I needed as a mother and helped me with organization for the family schedule. I love the fact that it is a continuous workbook that you can edit and change as life changes quickly. I am a mother of two children with a third on the way and with this workbook it allowed me to be able to find quality time to spend with my children. I highly recommend the TLC Workbook. I will be using this for the rest of my life and updating my weekly calendar as needed. I absolutely am in love with this and will also use it in my future career."

— Courtney Mendoza, Basic Counseling Skills Student

"In this TLC Workbook, Belinda Terro Mooney has done a fabulous job in creating a concrete, organized and practical guide for those (in fact, most or all of us) who need to improve their quality of life. More importantly, it has profound spiritual and psychological wisdom that sees the human person in his or her entirety as capable of achieving wholesome and healthy fulfillment in life."

—Virginia Fraguio, MA, Director of Faith Formation, St. Joseph Parish, Houston, Tx

Introduction

One day, as I was on my way to teach class, a former student saw me walking by and asked me to stop for a moment. His wife, who was on the phone with him, wanted to speak to me. He put her on speaker, and she said "Thank you for what you taught Leonard in your class! Because of you, he's really listening to me for the first time in our marriage!"

Leonard and I had practiced good listening techniques as part of his Basic Counseling Skills class. In writing goals for his Therapeutic Lifestyle Changes Workbook, he had made it a goal under Relationships to listen to his wife more deeply. He followed through with this TLC and his marriage began to thrive. I was thrilled to hear this news from his wife firsthand.

Therapeutic Lifestyle Changes (TLCs) are a commonsense approach to self-care that, when combined with therapy or medication, can facilitate healing in the brain and body. These changes made in key wellness areas of one's life help prevent burnout and promote health. They include spiritual enhancement, physical activity and exercise, sleep, nutrition, relationships, service, brain work, practicing hopeful thinking, emotional regulation, creative endeavors, and areas of self-discipline.

As a young professional, I worked 10 chaotic years while not practicing TLCs, and I burned out and caused harm to my body, resulting in chronic fatigue. I left the field to homeschool my children for 25 years. On my return, I began teaching at Lone Star College Montgomery Campus, where I was encouraged to see that TLCs had become standard practice in wellness and counseling.

I wanted to help my Basic Counseling Skills students create healthful habits that would allow them to flourish in their careers as helping professionals without burning out, and to provide a tool to help their clients. I created a basic TLC template with status, goals, and strengths in different areas. The original form has since been expanded to create Chapter 4 of this workbook. During a few months of the semester, students would fill in this form to set goals in each area of wellness, turn in their drafts for my input, and then revise and resubmit. My students' responses to using this tool were overwhelmingly positive. Before they even finished identifying and writing down goals in all TLC areas, they started feeling the effects of changes they had just begun to put into practice. Instead of orally describing how to fill in their TLCs, I wanted to include detailed written instructions, which became the first three chapters of this workbook. I soon realized that this format would benefit not only my students and their future clients but many health-conscious individuals and those in recovery as well.

If you long to heal your brain and body and to create a calm, stable lifestyle, this workbook is for you.

I've tried to keep the first three chapters as short and simple as possible so you can get right to Chapter 4 and begin writing your TLCs, implementing changes, and seeing results.

Let's get started!

1

Therapeutic Lifestyle Changes

Therapeutic Lifestyle Changes (TLCs) are lifestyle changes you can make in key areas (such as relationships, exercise, and sleep) that can make a dramatic, positive difference in your life. They have come to be regarded in the medical and human services fields as critical to helping people prevent and recover from illness and build resilience. TLCs are quickly becoming an essential part of the helping professions and being "prescribed" to help people lead healthy and productive lives. Optimal implementation of TLCs helps people feel happy and fulfilled and assists them in reaching their potential. Along with educating clients about new discoveries in neuroscience, helping them implement a comprehensive program of TLCs has become essential to therapeutic practice. The National Institutes of Health has even done a modified TLC program using diet, exercise, and weight management to help lower cholesterol.

Who can benefit from making Therapeutic Lifestyle Changes? The short answer is everyone who wants to order, balance, and improve the quality of their life. TLCs are especially helpful for people in recovery from trauma, addiction, codependency, and grief. Through my work with students, I've found that TLCs are a wonderful tool for current and aspiring professional counselors, social workers, and psychologists. Implementing TLCs can help prevent burnout, build clients' trust that you practice what you preach ("walk the walk"), and allow you to assist them more effectively in creating their own TLCs.

A variety of terms have been used to describe these wellness-focused areas of lifestyle changes. The TLCs I have developed in this book are a fairly comprehensive and representative sample.

This chapter focuses on describing each TLC area. Subsequent chapters help you create and implement comprehensive TLCs (including how to write out goals) to create the long-lasting habits that will allow you to maintain balance and to prevent relapse.

Spiritual Enhancement

Spiritual enhancement includes study of and reflection on your values and how you live by them. It also includes reflection on what you believe about the God of your understanding (Higher Power). Regardless of your religion or lack of one, having a Higher Power is key to recovery, as evidenced in 12-step recovery programs. Alcoholics Anonymous views a Higher Power as something greater than oneself, such as God or trust in the accountability and support of the group, to which one can relinquish control.

Spiritual enhancement can have a profound impact on your life. Being able to hand over control to God or a Higher Power is a great relief, as it can help you acknowledge that you can't handle all of your burdens alone. This aligns with the third step in 12-step programs ("Made a decision to turn our will and our lives over to the care of God as we understood Him").

Spiritual retreats, study, reflection, daily prayer, and meditation can help you build your relationship with God or your Higher Power. These activities may also help you reflect on how you see this relationship influencing your life. Seeing the connection can help you identify and prioritize your core values and the strengths you need to gain to help you live by those values. Making sure you live by your values can help you ensure integrity and peace within.

You can pray and meditate indoors or outdoors, in nature, or simply while walking down the street. An example would be to read a meditation or inspirational book before you leave, and then, as you walk, ponder what you've read. If you want to meditate without a book, you could reflect on the beauty of nature while you walk. Study is also important to building the relationship with your Higher Power. You might read books, attend a Bible study if you're

Christian, watch YouTube videos, listen to podcasts, or attend educational programs on spiritual topics.

Relationships

Having healthy relationships with others is important, but sometimes taken for granted. International best-selling author Matthew Kelly speaks of the importance of "carefree timelessness" in which you are so mentally and emotionally focused on the people you're with that you lose your sense of time. Pursuing carefree timelessness in healthy relationships can help you feel connected, appreciated, and fulfilled instead of lonely and isolated.

I have grouped interpersonal relationships into four categories: family, social, support group, and romantic.

Family

Depending on the mental and emotional health or illness of your family members, your family can be a positive or negative influence on your life. If your family is stable and you feel supported, you may want to connect with them more often. However, if you are not treated well or you consistently feel drained after interacting with them, setting boundaries may be the best option. In the midst of all your important relationships, you may find yourself taking family members for granted when they should be the ones you treat the best. Also, if you are married or in a committed relationship, with or without children, you have certain responsibilities and obligations. All of these are things to consider to get the most out of family relationships and to give appropriately as well.

Note: If you are in a domestic violence situation, please seek help from your local domestic violence center to carefully plan how to protect yourself (and your children).

Social

People need social relationships of all kinds to be well balanced. Your social relationships may involve neighbors, colleagues, and church and community friends. Improving your social skills and being a good friend can mean becoming a better listener, being aware of your role in a relationship, or achieving reciprocity. It is good to have a wide variety of social activities that you can regularly engage in to stay connected and prevent isolation. However, to stay balanced, it is important to not let one type of social relationship lead you to neglect others. You can create TLCs to help you balance the time you spend cultivating each relationship.

Support Group

Support groups can be helpful for anyone after a difficult event or major life change. For instance, a grief group may help with the grieving process after the death of a loved one. Support groups can be especially helpful when you're recovering from any kind of addiction or the effects of loving someone who is an addict. Bill W. and Dr. Bob developed the 12 steps, a revolutionary approach to addiction recovery, and formed Alcoholics Anonymous as the first 12-step support group. There are now many groups based on the 12 steps, including Narcotics Anonymous (NA) for people who use drugs other than alcohol, and Cocaine Anonymous (CA) for people whose drug of choice is cocaine.

Through all of these types of support groups, people with addictions get support and encouragement to stay abstinent (clean) one day at a time. You can do this through going to meetings and working through the 12 steps with a sponsor who gives you feedback and encouragement.

You can change your thoughts from "stinking thinking" to align with the steps and slogans, which can help retrain your brain. For example, the slogan "One day at a time" can help you worry less about trying to stay sober forever, as you only need to do it for today. Pressure and worry are detriments to sobriety, so using the slogans consistently provides a coping mechanism that becomes second nature when you are in a tight spot.

For family members or close friends of an addict, there are groups such as Al-Anon, Nar-Anon, and Codependents Anonymous. These groups help people recover from the effects of a loved one's addiction. Attendees learn to set boundaries and detach from the addict's problems while maintaining love for them.

Romantic

Romantic relationships can contribute greatly to your overall fulfillment or they can cause stress if not approached properly. A healthy romantic relationship should increase your happiness and enjoyment of life.

If you aren't currently dating but would like to do so, look for someone who will help and support you in maintaining balance. If you are in a committed relationship or have a loving spouse, a great goal for this TLC area would be learning to listen more deeply to improve and increase your communication. Consider what would help you develop your romantic life and allow you to increase your fulfillment and enjoyment with your partner.

A supportive partner or spouse can also be a great help to your recovery or aid you in preventing burnout. It is important to spend a quality time with your significant other to cultivate respect, affection, and trust. However, don't neglect your other relationships. Sometimes romantic partners can become too possessive and induce guilt when you try to maintain other relationships. (This can become abusive. You may want to talk to a friend, family member, or someone at a domestic violence center in your area). Remember, if your romantic relationship is causing you stress, take a step back and reevaluate it.

Service

Service is simply recognizing a need and moving to fulfill it. It can involve helping out in your community, at your place of worship, or with friends. Though not commonly thought of as service, intentional acts of kindness such as smiling, being calm, speaking in a gentle tone of voice, and not being in a hurry are all things that make a difference to those around you.

How do you want to be of service? Which people do you feel inspired to help most? How could you make a positive difference in the world? For example, if you want to volunteer with an organization such as Habitat for Humanity, you need to contact the local chapter, sign up, and schedule time to devote to its projects. You may want to help at a local domestic violence center or serve in a soup kitchen. Pick one or two avenues of service in this TLC area.

Cultural Identity

Having a strong connection to your cultural identity can help you identify with the strengths of your culture. By claiming these strengths, you can move beyond the damaging effects of others' racism, prejudice, and hatred. Consider focusing on developing relationships with people in your cultural group.

Learning about past and present heroes in your culture could help you see how you might apply cultural influences to enhance your life. Reading about your culture, learning your native language, and studying the history of your culture can help you further understand and be proud of your roots. This TLC can increase your self-respect, your sense of community, and understanding of your strengths.

Exercise

Exercise is important for so many health reasons, yet you may find it difficult to fit into a busy schedule. It may become easier if you begin to feel the tremendous difference exercise can make in your overall well-being, your brain functionality, and your body. You most likely need a highly specific goal in this TLC area so you can get consistent activity and start experiencing the benefits, which will motivate you to continue with your plan.

Dr. John Ratey, author of *Spark: The Revolutionary New Science of Exercise and the Brain*, has done extensive reviews of literature to highlight the beneficial effects of exercise on the brain as well as the rest of the body. His findings indicate that starting a comprehensive regimen of exercise as a TLC can alleviate depression and combat illness. If you're depressed, exercise can help stabilize your brain by releasing endorphins and increasing dopamine and serotonin levels. If you're in recovery from trauma or any type of substance use disorder or addiction, exercise can greatly aid your healing by helping you release anger and other triggering emotions.

Aerobic exercise helps the heart and muscles. Weight-bearing exercise and strength training build muscle and strengthen bones. Swimming is an excellent exercise for the brain and body because it combines aerobics and stretch training. When a swimmer dies, if an autopsy is done and their brain is examined, the doctors can tell that they were a swimmer because their brain tissue is so healthy!

Stretch training is also highly beneficial. It releases tension and helps you feel better in general. In the book *Stretching Anatomy,* Arnold Nelson and Jouko Kokkonen state, "Additional research has shown that regular, intense stretching for a minimum of 10 minutes will bring some major beneficial changes in the neuromuscular-tendon units." They state that this results in an increase in strength, endurance, flexibility, and mobility.

There are many options for intense stretching. Pilates was originally developed for the rehabilitation of soldiers. Barre, which combines elements of ballet and Pilates, is a more active and high-impact option. Callanetics, which focuses on contracting specific muscle groups, is low impact. Yoga techniques and postures stem from Buddhist spirituality. Pietra Fitness incorporates Christian meditation.

Sleep

Sleep is critical to maintaining the health of your brain and body. You need sleep in order to let your brain create new neural pathways (interconnected neurons). Rest also helps your muscles relax and takes the stress off of your bones, which have been in an upright position all day. Like relaxation, sleep refreshes you so you can work more effectively and be more focused.

The human body goes through 90-minute sleep cycles, with initial sleepiness coming around sunset and wakefulness returning close to sunrise. According to Dr. Nerina Ramlakhan in her book, *Tired But Wired: The Essential Sleep Toolkit*, the hours of sleep you get before 12 a.m. are the most beneficial (especially the 90-minute sleep cycle from 10:30 p.m. to 12 a.m.). This particular cycle is the most instrumental in the processing of long-term memories and the restoration of the body. If you regularly miss this cycle, you may find yourself consistently tired, even if you sleep 8–9 hours after midnight. Research on people with Alzheimer's disease shows that people who are sleep deprived for long periods of time or work shifts opposite to the circadian rhythm are most at risk for the disease. So, if you stay up at all hours and don't get adequate sleep, you can increase your risk of getting Alzheimer's.

Do you tend to push yourself to get work done and not get enough sleep? Do you rationalize not sleeping with "I have so much to do?" If poor sleep is a continual problem for you, consider getting an evaluation for depression (depression often affects sleep patterns) or a formal sleep study to help determine whether you have a medical problem such as sleep apnea.

Sleep as a TLC includes factors like getting enough hours of rest, sleeping in a quiet atmosphere, and having any necessary equipment, such as a white noise machine, a favorite pillow, or a comfortable mattress. Some people, especially if their sleep has been disturbed for a long time, benefit from taking supplements such as magnesium or melatonin, which are natural sleep aids.

How many hours of sleep do you really need and what are you willing to do to get them? Start with what time you need to get up in the morning and work backward. If you must be up by 7 a.m. and you need 8 hours of sleep, then you must be asleep by 11 p.m. Factor in the length of your bedtime routine to determine what time you need to be in bed and fully relaxed in order to fall asleep. Figure it out, implement specific techniques, and make this goal a priority. After a few weeks, your body will feel the difference.

Nutrition

Food

Nutrition can be confusing because there is so much advice on how to "eat healthy" that people do not know what to believe. Multitudes of foods are considered good or bad, and these labels often depend on which diet plan you might be following. Diets are regimented, strict, and merciless, allowing for little to no flexibility. The difficulty of staying on a diet is one reason that *98% of diets do not work.* Diet plans are usually based on forcing the body to go into ketogenesis (starvation mode). However, humans are not meant to starve, so at some point, people who diet begin eating "normally" again. When they take up eating "forbidden" foods again, they may overindulge. Eventually, they gain back their lost weight, and they are once again caught in a cycle of shame, anxiety, and stress. According to eating disorder specialists, the "diet culture" that focuses on weight loss is highly toxic and can actually further disordered eating habits.

What can you do? Try implementing balanced eating habits and an active lifestyle. With that kind of goal, you can focus less on losing weight and more on feeling satisfied, nourished, and refreshed. To eat in a balanced way and prevent disordered eating habits, eating disorder specialists generally recommend the thirds rule. Divide your plate in thirds. Fill one third with protein, one third with vegetables or fruit, and one third with grains. One or two of these segments can include some type of fat, such as cheese, butter, or salad dressing. At breakfast (or with at least one meal), it's good to have some dairy products (if you are allergic to dairy or lactose intolerant, you can substitute a nut-based milk such as almond milk). If you're allergic to gluten, you can substitute grains like rice for wheat. Occasionally, when you are not already full, you might have dessert after a meal.

If you worry that you are overweight, obese, or too thin, consult a nutritionist. You may be struggling with an eating disorder. If this is the case, dieting will only make the problem worse. A nutritionist who understands eating disorders can help you stop worrying, bingeing, and restricting your food intake and will treat the cause rather than the symptoms.

Hydration

Water is so important to humans' brains and bodies, yet, as with sleep deprivation, many of us are dehydrated. Our very survival depends upon having water as a sustaining force similar to good foods. With proper hydration, you can stay energized and your body can function well with less likelihood of having health problems such as kidney stones. Adequate water intake can also reduce inflammation brought on by stress, as well as keep your skin smooth and youthful-looking. The current recommendation from nutritionists is 4–6 16-ounce glasses per day.

An easy way to stay hydrated is to drink one full glass of water upon rising and before breakfast, and another throughout the day as you feel thirsty. Bring a water bottle to school and work. If you are exercising, make sure to hydrate periodically.

Health

Physical

Have you been neglecting some area of your physical health? How long ago was your last physical exam and blood work? How about the dentist or optometrist? Are there appointments you can't seem to get around to scheduling? This workbook can help you carve out the time and gather the courage to do the health-maintenance-related things you've been putting off.

Mental and Emotional

The goal of creating a TLC based on your mental and emotional needs is to help you improve your self-awareness, manage and minimize distressing thoughts, and regulate emotions so that you can live a happier, more emotionally healthy life.

Do you have anxiety, depression, an eating disorder, or post-traumatic stress affecting your life but you've stopped your medical or therapy appointments? Scheduling an appointment to see a psychiatrist, psychologist or other therapist, nutritionist, eating-disorder specialist, or trauma specialist trained in EMDR could give you hope and help you become more resilient.

Are you living in an abusive situation and feeling stuck, or afraid you would be in danger if you tried to leave or ask for change in your situation? The people at a local domestic violence center would keep your situation confidential and could be a great source of support in helping you identify your choices. (See the Bibliography and Extra Reading list at the back of this workbook for the National Domestic Violence Hotline.)

Therapy, 12-step work, and TLCs can help you regulate your emotions. Journaling in particular has been proven to be effective in improving self-awareness and handling distressing emotions. According to one therapist I know personally, people who journal typically recover from trauma *twice as quickly* as people who don't.

You don't have to like writing in order to journal, and journaling does not have to be done in a specific way. Many people prefer drawing pictures to writing. Some people find that writing fiction helps them deal with emotional issues. Regardless of what form of journaling you do, you will likely make many discoveries about yourself in the process. For example, if someone labeled you as selfish when you were growing up, journaling about this situation and how it impacted you may help you see that the *person who labeled you* was really the selfish one and projecting their feelings on you. Then, in the future if you are tempted to believe the negative label, you can think to yourself, "I am *not* selfish, that was *your* problem."

Self-soothing is a form of emotional regulation: you calm yourself by engaging one or more of your senses in something pleasant. You might light a scented candle and listen to calming music while reading a good book, or sit outdoors and meditate while listening to the birds. Self-soothing can also help before working on recommendations from a therapist or doing step work. It can help you stay calm while navigating the hassles of daily life, and it is especially helpful for recovering from trauma.

Work/Finances

Work can be stressful, to say the least. Sometimes it is energizing and sometimes it is overwhelming. What can you do to manage your time at work and preserve your work/life balance? You can communicate with your supervisor to understand what needs to be done and when, then write down due dates and plan how to meet your deadlines. Try to schedule your time so you can go home at the end of the day and leave your work at the office, knowing you did the best you could.

Finances can also be difficult to manage properly, especially if you struggle to make enough money. This workbook may give you the push you need to manage your time at work and your finances so you can decrease your stress levels.

Brain Work

Neurobics

Getting enough intellectual stimulation may be an important TLC for you. If you want to increase the capacity of certain parts of your brain, I want to challenge you to *work consistently on having a calm lifestyle,* which can help your brain function at its highest capacity and help you heal emotionally from any trauma. According to Dr. Vincent Fortanasce in his book *The Anti-Alzheimer's Prescription,* anything that helps our brains function better can also help prevent Alzheimer's disease.

Dr. Edward Hallowell, who helps people with neurological problems, refers to exercise done specifically for the brain as "Neurobics." You can do some simple and fun exercises such as Sudoku, word finds, crossword puzzles, and logic puzzles. These are all excellent activities for keeping your brain active and stimulating it. Chess, which has been called "the ultimate game" because of the way it employs the strategic areas of the brain, is another option.

Also, consider doing some type of math for 20 minutes and then playing music later in the day. Dr. Martin Bergee of the University of Kansas has found that when people regularly practice math and music on the same day, they improve their skills in both areas more than when they practice only one. This combination, since it engages both sides of the brain, stimulates the brain to reach its greatest overall productivity.

Higher Education

Being organized at school is one of the most important things you can do for yourself. As a student, you can greatly increase your sense of order, peace, and calm if you create a plan to keep up with your assignments. One thing you could do is write out a weekly plan for how you are going to get everything done by the due dates. Then write out the amount of reading, writing, and research you need for each assignment according to the number of days you have. Put this on a calendar with reminders. This plan has worked very well for many students.

Creativity

Creativity is regarded as the mark of a flourishing civilization because art and creativity are part of our innermost beings as humans. Scientifically speaking, creative pursuits stimulate the right side of the brain, keeping it healthy and active. If you are not currently engaging in any creative activities, try to make time to do at least one creative thing, such as working on a hobby, each week. You will likely find your life more enjoyable and relaxing as a result.

Attending concerts and visiting museums are good ways to appreciate fine arts. Playing a musical instrument and singing are intensely creative activities. Reading books or writing your own can help you get in touch with your innermost self. Fine arts, such as drawing and painting, are things that many people find particularly relaxing that you might want to explore as well.

If fine arts are not your thing, you might prefer a hobby such as woodworking or repairing old cars. Or you could try styling hair and learning new makeup techniques. Perhaps photography, videography, or cooking can get your creative juices flowing. Pick something and start making time for discovering your talents!

Self-Discipline

Screen Time

Whether you're scrolling through Instagram feeds, checking Facebook, or watching YouTube videos, looking at a screen can be the ultimate time killer. Checking out what your friends are doing or simply having a good laugh are not bad things to do, per se, but spending too much time on them can cause an imbalance in how you spend the rest of your time, as well as make you less productive.

It is important to monitor how much time you spend in front of a screen. Too much time can result in this becoming an addictive activity. Even if you have a computer-based job, you can do two things. First, distinguish between your computer time for work and your computer time for recreation. Set boundaries for when you are working and when you aren't so that you keep these segments separate. Stay focused while you are researching a work project instead of getting sidetracked looking up something else. Save leisure-time activity for later. That way, you know you will get to it eventually, but it will not interrupt your current activity. This will increase your productivity and help you more effectively manage your screen time. If you must spend a lot of time looking at a screen, consider taking 5-minute breaks from looking at a screen every so often. Walk around, stretch, maybe get a glass of water, and don't think about anything work or screen related. These actions can help you ensure that you maintain self-discipline with screen time.

Alcohol and Other Drugs

According to Alcoholics Anonymous and Al-Anon, alcoholism is a disease that runs in families and has a strong genetic component. So, if your close relatives, especially your parents, struggle or struggled with alcohol dependency, your risk of becoming an alcoholic is high. You may want to consider abstaining from alcohol as the safest course of action. Do not make the common mistake of thinking that you can be the one in your family to show others how to drink alcohol properly. It is better to be proactive and make a commitment to not drink now rather than get caught on a slippery slope.

Even if alcoholism does not run in your family, it's still smart to be cautious when drinking. *Never get drunk.* Getting drunk is the first major step in the progression toward developing dependency and addiction. Implement good practices when you drink. At the beginning of an event where you'll be drinking, determine roughly how many drinks you'll have. Stick to it. If you're at a social event and your weight is average, 2–3 drinks in the course of a longer night might be a good standard. Never drive when you drink more than is legally allowed in a certain time frame. Drink with friends who do not abuse alcohol, and, especially if you're a woman, don't let other people get drinks for you. All of this will help you stay accountable to the plan you set up at the beginning of the night. If you find yourself consistently not following your plan and beginning to have problems in your life, you can seek an assessment from a licensed chemical dependency counselor (LCDC) before you progress further.

Smoking

Smoking is the number-one preventable cause of death. There are absolutely no health benefits to smoking, and there are many risks. By stopping the risks of cancer, COPD, and other respiratory illnesses, you can immediately start to improve your health and longevity.

Of course, quitting smoking is much easier said than done. This workbook provides some resources so you can create an effective, personalized plan to quit.

Practical Tip: Making Adjustments

Sometimes you can implement TLCs by adjusting things you already do. For example, one of my students used to read a book while having coffee in the morning before work, but she was not meditating or doing enough exercise. To add in some meditation time, she switched some things around. Now she reads and ponders her AA meditation book in the morning while sipping her coffee. Later, when she goes home to walk the dog, she listens to an audio book for brain stimulation and walks the dog for a longer time. She gets in two TLCs (brain work and exercise) while taking care of her dog, and she can also meditate. She can succeed in maintaining her new plan because she started with what she already had in place—drinking coffee and walking the dog—and just rearranged her activities.

You want to reach goals, but sometimes you get sidetracked in the process (perhaps you make too many commitments), and setting up the right TLCs could be just what you need to solve the problem. This workbook is designed to assist you in identifying and implementing *all* your TLCs so that you can lead a more balanced life. It is action-oriented to help you start being more productive, creating healthy habits, and accomplishing your goals.

2

Identifying Current Status, Goals, Strengths, and Resources

In Chapter 4, where you'll develop your TLCs, you'll write down what you're doing or not doing in a given area (current status), what you want to do (projected goal), and who or what can help you do it (inner strengths and external resources).

Current Status: What I Am and Am Not Doing

Your current status is simply what you are doing in any given area, even if it's nothing. If you have fallen out of a good habit, don't worry; it is quite common for people to neglect certain areas of their well-being. Observing and noting what you're doing or not doing can help you reflect on the situation and then decide what steps you want to take next.

When you write down what you're doing, note whether you are being consistent about it. Think about your patterns and obstacles. If you know why things have not worked, such as why you stopped exercising after only two weeks, state it.

If you have no exercise program at the moment, for current status, write something like "I do not have an exercise plan or regimen yet" or "I tried going to the gym but got discouraged and gave up." If you do something regularly, you might write "I currently run 3 times a week on Mondays, Wednesdays, and Fridays, right after work, at 5:30." Note any inconsistency: "I try to run 3 times per week but mostly do it only on Wednesday and Friday."

Under Nutrition, you might write "I do not currently eat three meals a day." If you do eat three meals, you might write "I eat three meals a day but am not consistent with meal times."

Under Self-Discipline with Screen Time, when noting your status, distinguish between necessary work or school-related time and leisure time spent on your computer or cell phone. You could write "I use my personal computer for 3–4 hours daily for school work. I am on the computer or my phone for an additional 2 hours for other reasons." If you would prefer to spend less leisure time using screens to make time for activities that you are neglecting, then later, under Projected Goals, you can specify a plan.

Projected Goals (Specific Things You Will Do)

Your projected goals are what you want to accomplish. To be achievable, they must be specific. Writer Antoine De Saint-Exupery said, "A goal without a plan is just a wish." I encourage you to be extremely specific with your goals. "I want to increase the amount of exercise I do" is not specific enough. "I will swim laps Tuesday, Thursday, and Saturday from 6 to 7 a.m. at the YMCA" is much better.

I want to repeat this because it is so easy to be vague when setting goals: Remember to be extremely specific with your projected goals. You will not be able to achieve a goal unless it is specific.

Goals should be realistic, observable, and measurable.

Realistic. I mean this in the sense that you can do it, or part of it, *now*, rather than needing to make many substantive life changes. Setting a goal to walk five times a week to start may not be realistic if you don't have walking time in your schedule now, and especially if you have appointments and activities that you need to rearrange before you can succeed. In this case, it is better to write something like "I will walk twice per week on Tuesday and Thursday at 3:30 p.m. beginning tomorrow."

If your ultimate goal is to walk five times per week, you can create a plan that gets you to that point over time. Each step of the overall goal should be realistic. For instance, you could start with the goal "I will walk twice per week on Tuesday and Thursday at 3:30 p.m., beginning tomorrow." You could continue with something like "I will maintain this schedule for one month. Then I will increase walking to 3 times per week (Tuesday, Thursday, and Saturday) for an additional 2 months. After 3 months, I will walk 5 times per week, on Sunday, Tuesday, Thursday, Friday, and Saturday." Rather than trying to radically change everything in your life to immediately get you to your ultimate goal (which could create an imbalance in other ways), this type of plan gives you enough time to shift your activities around.

Observable and measurable. You need to be able to monitor and assess your progress. This is why planning is so important. For instance, with walking, do not take a chance on remembering when a month is up to add in your Saturday walks. Plan it and write it down. Putting everything on your calendar, setting reminders on your phone, and staying organized will help you attain your goals.

For nutrition and exercise TLCs, you may want to make your first goal scheduling an appointment with a nutritionist, doctor, or personal trainer to get input on appropriate goals. For TLCs related to emotions and spirituality, finding a therapist or sponsor is a good first goal.

Writing down a goal that you subsequently review can improve your chances of achieving it. For example, write: "I will find a good therapist and schedule an appointment by the end of this week." Then put a reminder on your digital calendar.

If you've been neglecting physical fitness for a long time, you may need to start with something like physical therapy or chiropractic visits. For your goal, break down the steps to getting that help.

For example: "I will schedule an appointment with my primary care physician by Thursday to get a referral to a physical therapist. I will schedule the appointment with the physical therapist (or wait for the doctor's office to do it), and then I will keep that appointment. I will follow every recommendation with a reminder on my phone and daily checklist for accountability."

For your TLC areas for which the current status is sufficient, simply state under Projected Goals, "I will continue to [insert current habit]."

Look at each area of your life that needs attention and set a goal for it that is realistic, observable, and measurable. Set goals to achieve in a week or a month and review them regularly. You might review them weekly at first, then monthly after you have succeeded in solidifying healthy habits in all the areas.

Spiritual Enhancement Goals

Spiritual goals might be something like "I will have an attitude of gratitude for everything that God or my Higher Power is doing in my life. On Sunday afternoons, I will list the things I am grateful for in the past week and remember all the good things that happened. I have placed my gratitude journal next to my meditation chair with a pen. I will practice feeling hopeful about the good things to come in the week I'm beginning, and write down good things at night when I review my day."

Another spiritual goal might be "Before I go to bed every night, I will do a review. I will look back on my day, see where I could have done better according to my values and goals, and say 'thank you' to my Higher Power for all the good things that happened. I have set a reminder on my phone to help me build this habit."

Relationship Goals

Do you have a TLC related to maintaining your family and social relationships? Perhaps you want to call one person once per week to maintain your connection. You might set a goal such as "On Wednesday nights after dinner, I will call my old friends from California," or "On Sunday afternoons, I will call my mom or one of my siblings."

Other relationship goals might include:

"I will go out with a group of friends on Saturdays, making sure to stick to my goal of alcohol discipline (see below) by calling an accountability partner beforehand."

"On Tuesdays and Thursdays, I will spend time after class with friends who help me be the best version of myself."

"I will schedule lunch with one friend each week on Wednesday from 11 a.m. to noon."

For family relationships: "I will schedule one-on-one time with my kids on Saturday and Sunday between 2 and 4 p.m., giving each child their own special time" or "On rainy days, I will dance with the children to our favorite music in the living room."

Goals related to support group or sponsor relationships might be plans such as: "I will continue to show up for support group meetings. On Fridays at lunch, I will call my sponsor and update her on my recovery."

For a romantic relationship, you might write: "I will schedule dates with my boyfriend for every Friday night" or "I will schedule date night with my spouse on the last Friday of the month at 7 p.m."

If you already have certain goals set up, you can write something like, "I currently see friends 2–3 times per week on Wednesdays, Saturdays, and Sundays. I will continue to do so."

Service Goals

For intentional acts of kindness, you may want to make a goal like this: "I will give three people a genuine compliment today."

For service to society, sample goals could include, "I will keep a bag in the laundry room for clothing donations. I will donate clothes and home furnishings to the Domestic Violence Center Resale Shop every 3 months, at the end of March, June, September, and December. I have put the dates on my calendar."

"I will contact the local soup kitchen tomorrow at noon to inquire about volunteering. I will set further goals based on that conversation."

Cultural Identity Goals

Do you have a TLC goal for becoming acquainted with the history of your family and culture? A possible goal could be: "I will learn more about my culture. On Saturday evening around 7 p.m., for the next 4 weeks, I will research and explore my culture and genealogy on the Internet."

You might follow that goal with a continuation such as "To build a sense of community with others in my culture, I will find an online group that is dedicated to my cultural history and connect with it once a week, on Saturdays at 7 p.m."

Another possible goal: "I will talk to my children Sunday afternoon about our extended family and cultural background. I will teach them how to make a traditional meal."

Exercise Goals

Do *not* do yourself a disservice by writing "I have no exercise goals to achieve because I don't have time to exercise." Exercise is critically important for maintaining your physical health. You can set aside at least 20 minutes to exercise 4 times a week.

Designate days and times that work with what you already have on your schedule. When can you work out? Be specific about when you will exercise, on what days, at what time, and where.

Sample goals could include actions like: "I will take the stairs instead of the elevator when I go upstairs for class. That is twice on Monday, Wednesday, and Friday, and 3 times on Tuesday and Thursday."

Another goal: "I will walk on the nature trail every Tuesday and Sunday at 6 p.m. If I am sick, I will alter the days to be equivalent to two days for 30 minutes. On days with bad weather, I will do 30 minutes of deep stretching at home."

Or you might prefer, "I will go to the gym and consult a personal trainer about setting up a weight-lifting routine. I will go to the gym on Wednesday, Thursday, and Saturday from 8 to 9:00 a.m. After one month, I will evaluate my progress and set new goals. I have put these dates on my calendar."

Under Projected Goals, you can first state an overall goal, then a specific objective, for example:

General: "I will develop an exercise plan and begin tomorrow."

Specific: "I will exercise for one month 3 days per week on Monday, Wednesday, and Friday from 4 to 5 p.m. by walking or jogging, beginning tomorrow and ending on April 14. The second month (April 15 to May 14), I will continue exercising and add swimming on Tuesday, Thursday, and Saturday from 2–3 p.m. The third month (May 15 to June 14), I will continue as in the second month, then evaluate at the end of that time period and make any needed adjustments."

Sleep Goals

If you have problems getting to sleep or staying asleep, before writing down your goals, consider: What are your thoughts right before going to bed? Do you use your cell phone or computer, which stimulate brain activity, in bed or right before you go to sleep? Are you sporadic about the time you go to sleep and wake up?

Then set your goals accordingly:

"I will think thoughts of gratitude and practice deep breathing as I lie down at 10 p.m. I will set the alarm to wake me up at 6 a.m."

"I will use my bed for sleeping only, and watch movies elsewhere, so that when I walk toward my bed, my body will know it's time to relax."

"I will stop using my cell phone or computer at least an hour before I go to bed so that I can naturally calm down as bedtime nears. I have set a timer on my phone."

If your sleep times are sporadic, scheduling a half-hour routine of getting ready for bed in which you journal, pray, stretch, or generally relax can be effective in helping your mind and body prepare for sleep. Something as simple as turning on a white noise machine can signal your brain that it's time to sleep. A possible goal could be, "I will make my bedtime preparation experience as pleasant as possible by engaging multiple senses. I will light a scented candle, play calming music, and do a little stretching. I will turn on white noise right before I get in bed."

Another might be, "I will establish a rhythm by being in bed by 11 p.m. and getting out of bed by 7 a.m." or "In the next 3 days, I will develop a sleep routine to get ready for bed. I will stop watching movies by 9 p.m., take melatonin, and quietly read from 9 to 10 p.m. or until I feel really tired."

Nutrition Goals

Being stressed out can lead to craving high-calorie foods in response to your body's perception that it might need to fight or flee. When you are stressed out, you may tend toward emotional eating, such as consuming foods high in sugar rather than more balanced options. While carbohydrates are a necessity for fuel, an excess of anything is not good.

Our omnivorous diets should contain a bit of everything. So, good goals could be plans like "I will eat cake or drink soda only on Sundays, and I will have satisfying, healthy snacks on hand for when I get cravings at other times. On Sunday, I will pack 5 protein bars in my backpack for the next week for a good snack option that effectively satisfies my hunger." Another might be "I will eat fruits and vegetables daily at breakfast and dinner. I will plan and shop for meals on Saturday to make sure I have enough healthy options for the week."

If you currently skip breakfast, a good goal would be to make sure that you have something every morning: "By Saturday, I will look up recipes for easy smoothies for a great no-mess drink on the way to work or class, beginning on Monday."

Another goal might be, "I will try one new nutritionally balanced recipe each week on Friday night. I will look for a recipe on Sunday afternoon as I relax, and make the dish the following Friday."

Other goals could include "I will create a standing grocery shopping list that includes plenty of fruits and vegetables. I will cook and eat at least one vegetable with lunch and one with dinner."

To consume consistent amounts of calories throughout the day, try to keep your meals evenly spaced. If you eat sporadically, establishing consistent meal times would help.

Because anxiety can increase with caffeine intake, maybe consider how you could limit your caffeine. It's better to drink water than coffee (and if you continually need coffee, this is a good indicator that what you *really* need is better sleep! Go back to your goals for sleep and work on this area.)

If you are deficient in certain nutrients or vitamins, or want to boost your immune system, consider taking supplements. Sample goals could include "I will take a multivitamin with breakfast beginning Thursday; I will get the vitamins at the store Wednesday afternoon. I will put them on my placemat or set a reminder on my phone so I don't forget."

For staying hydrated, you might write, "I will drink 4–6 16-oz. glasses of water a day. Eight ounces in the morning just after I get up, a full glass with each meal, and 8 ounces mid-morning, mid-afternoon, and after dinner. I will set a reminder if I cannot remember. I will bring a water bottle to work and refill it during the day."

Physical Health Goals

It's important to keep your medical check-ups regular to avoid complications. Scheduling them in advance, all at once, is typically the best way to stay on top of this. A sample goal might be: "I will schedule all my medical exams (annual physical, gynecological, and eye exam), as well as a dental exam every 6 months. I will put them on my calendar and set reminders on my phone."

Mental and Emotional Health Goals

A TLC could be something like: "I will search for a good therapist, find one, and contact them to make an appointment by this Friday at 4 p.m.

Another: "I will listen to David Burns' *Feeling Good: The New Mood Therapy*" every morning as I drive to work.

For realistic, hopeful thinking, you could set a goal like "I will allow myself thinking time. I will spend time thinking about things and making adjustments. I will practice hopeful thinking 30 minutes a day as I go for a walk at about 5 p.m. when I get home."

Another way to do it: "Sunday is a good day to spend time thinking. I will go on a long walk after I finish running at 4 p.m. and just sit in the park by the water and think about and plan my life. I will identify any negative thoughts that bothered me in the preceding week and journal about them. I will set a goal to replace those thoughts with new, positive thoughts and affirmations in my journal, and put them in my phone. I will look over my TLCs and see how I'm doing."

You could also simply write "At the end of every day, I will pay attention to what went right and list 3 things I'm thankful for."

A couple more:

"I will replace negative thoughts about myself with true and hopeful thoughts, such as 'I am a beloved child of God' or 'I can and I will overcome fear. I can do this new thing one step at a time.'"

To regulate your emotions through your behavior, you can strive to build space between your emotions and reactions, which can help you avoid making damaging decisions. Notice when your emotions are controlling your behavior. Pause and take a break, and wait until they do not control your behavior. In the AA tradition, use the acronym HALT—are you too hungry, angry, lonely, tired?

Sample goals might include: "I will practice getting in touch with my emotions by setting a timer three times a day (morning, noon, and night) to notice how I've been feeling in the past few hours and how I've reacted or responded to those feelings. I will keep my journal with me and record all my difficult emotions. I will discuss these with God or my Higher Power at the end of the day and with my therapist or sponsor during the week." Writing, especially journaling or writing people letters you don't intend to mail, is an excellent way to get out your emotions.

Other ideas:

"I will work on developing a sense of humor by watching a funny video while I get ready for work at 7 a.m."

"I will begin therapy within 2 weeks to deal with trauma I experienced at age 17."

"I will schedule my first session for anger-management therapy by next Friday."

"I will start attending Al-Anon ACOA meetings for my family-of-origin issues with parental (and relatives') alcohol abuse and dependence."

Another goal could be "I will journal for 15 minutes every night when I am relaxing and getting ready for bed. I will write down the things that make me feel stressed so I can have a clear mind when I go to sleep."

Or, if you have a friend who can encourage and uplift you, perhaps write: "I will ask [friend's name] if he/she wants to get lunch together regularly after class on Tuesdays. I will let him/her know if I'm not doing well so I can receive support."

For emotional regulation through relaxation ("me" time), perhaps find a place where someone is playing the piano or listen to calming music.

Just as you schedule time with family and friends, schedule alone time in your routine. Goals could include:

"I will take a hot bath on Saturday night (and short showers on other nights). I will have my oldest child watch the younger ones so that I won't be interrupted."

"I will do deep breathing exercises three times daily in conjunction with meditation in the morning and an emotional regulation check at noon and in the evening."

"I will go outside and breathe deeply every day at lunchtime."

Creativity Goals

Playing an instrument, singing, repairing a car, journaling, writing stories or poetry, drawing, painting, decorating your home, organizing, and even coloring are great ways to keep your brain healthy and regulate your emotions at the same time. Creative endeavors that help you handle your emotions, like using a coloring book, drawing, or journaling, count as two TLCs—creative and emotional.

Goals in the creative realm could include:

"I will take a drawing class at the community college this summer and draw at night 3 times a week."

"I will read one great book every 3 months. I have prioritized my list and will begin tomorrow with *The Silmarillion* by J.R.R. Tolkien."

Self-Discipline Goals: Screen Time

We've discussed necessary screen time as opposed to leisurely screen time. If being on a computer regularly results in your watching YouTube videos or browsing the web, you need to designate the amount of time you'll do each activity. If you're working, you should be completely focused on the work. Then, when you take a break, you can fully enjoy your leisure time. This will help you stay productive and get things done in an efficient manner.

A goal related to limiting your screen time could be something like: "After an hour of working, I will watch one short video or read one article. When I finish a bigger project or am finished for the day, I'll watch a movie."

Note: Rewarding yourself for hard work is productive. Letting yourself drift into another world when you need to do something important or meet a deadline is not, and your self-esteem will pay a high price if you come up short.

Perhaps you are on your phone and procrastinating out of fear or freezing up due to a past trauma, and you would be able to benefit from working with a therapist. This type of TLC can fall under Mental and Emotional Health Goals as well; you may want to have goals in both of these areas.

A sample goal might be: "On Friday at my 1 p.m. therapy session, I will explore my fear that results in playing on my phone to procrastinate.

Self-Discipline Goals: Alcohol and Drugs

If you are in recovery, you know to stay away from people, places, and things that trigger your urge to drink or use drugs and put you at high risk for relapse. Your goals might be plans such as:

"I will continue to abstain from drinking and using drugs."

"I will stay away from people, places, and things that trigger relapse."

"I will not attend parties with people, including family members, who drink too much or use drugs."

"I will develop a comprehensive relapse prevention plan with my sponsor or therapist."

If you don't think you're addicted to alcohol but at times you've felt uneasy about the amount or way you drink, you could set a TLC goal to attempt to stop drinking and observe what happens: "I will stop drinking for 3 months, observe my attitudes and behaviors, and seek input from trusted family members and friends."

At a minimum, you can set a goal that "I will not drink until I'm drunk. I will monitor my behavior on every occasion of drinking to see if I'm doing OK, and I will drink only with friends whom I have asked to give me feedback about my behavior."

Remember, getting drunk is the first step to alcohol dependency. For people who are just beginning to drink, an appropriate TLC goal could be "I will never get drunk." For most people of average weight, two to three drinks in the course of a night is enough to engage socially without becoming drunk. If you have had more than this and still believe you are not drunk or are "just a little high," be careful. People often minimize (try to believe or make others believe something isn't as bad as it really is) as they are heading toward alcoholism.

If you have a strong family history of chemical dependency (especially if both your parents were addicts), a goal could be "I will abstain from alcohol as a preventative measure for the sake of my health and my relationships with my family. I do not want to end up addicted because I believed that I was better than the addicts in my family and could show them how avoiding addiction is done."

Self-Discipline Goals: Quitting Smoking

Many people try to stop smoking for their health. However, quitting can be tremendously difficult if you do not set a specific TLC goal with a huge reward for succeeding. It is best to plan carefully and set up a series of deadlines for each step you take, as well as plan to implement coping strategies for when you stop.

Some people have goals such as "I will quit smoking on [date]." This gives you a definitive time frame for your ambitious commitment to change. However, your progress is not likely to be sustainable if you do not prepare for various challenges that you're likely to face after you stop smoking.

You need to replace the urge for nicotine with a positive habit. A possible goal could be "I will make a list of coping mechanisms that I can use and keep on hand to refer to when I have urges." Some people also find it helpful to include a list of reasons motivating them to stay clean. This list might include the well wishes of family members and friends or a goal you are putting in jeopardy with your chemical dependency. Try something like "I will make a concrete list of the reasons I have for living without smoking, post it (on my mirror, in my phone and computer) and look at it first thing in the morning and last thing at night."

Another sustainable goal might be, "I will write down a list of coping mechanisms and motivations during my Thursday session with my counselor. I will pin the list to my dream board to remind myself that smoking is not worth destroying my dream of having a happy, healthy life. I will refer to this list weekly and recommit to abstinence, and if I have urges to smoke, I will refer to it again *immediately*."

A good TLC would be something like, "I will have regularly scheduled appointments with a counselor" or "I will ask my sponsor to help with accountability and work the 12 steps for my smoking addiction." Like alcoholics, people in recovery from smoking need kindred souls who can help them on their journey. If you do not have a support group, write something like, "Tonight, instead of watching the news when I get home from work, I will locate and reach out to a support group that can help me stick to my commitment."

Note: Other Types of Addiction

If you struggle with another type of addition, such as gambling, viewing pornography, or playing video games, you can seek help for that as well. Possible goals could include, "I will attend Gamblers Anonymous meetings on Mondays and Fridays" or "I will install Covenant Eyes on the computer to block pornographic websites and get an accountability partner today," or "I will decrease my video game time to 1 hour per day and use the time I gain from that to pursue my other TLC areas."

Strengths and Resources to Help You Accomplish Your Goals

Strengths are your inner qualities, gifts, talents, and virtues, including your past successes. Your strengths can help you achieve your goals. Most strengths can be summed up in one or a few words, such as:

- Self-discipline
- Strong faith
- Desire
- Commitment
- Persistence
- Compassion
- Determination
- Self-control
- Consistency
- Prior or current successes
- Natural abilities and talents
- Loyalty
- Curiosity
- Intelligence
- Willingness to learn
- Technological aptitude
- Stability
- Social skills
- Extraversion or introversion
- Being a true friend
- Enthusiasm
- Optimism
- A sense of humor
- Common sense
- Athleticism

- A desire to maintain good health
- An ability to set and achieve goals
- Love of learning
- Love of art
- Love of your culture
- Motivation
- A good habit already formed

Resources are supportive people and organizations, groups, and literature, such as:

- God or a Higher Power
- Your family
- Reliable friends
- Strong relationships
- A caring partner/spouse
- A skilled sponsor
- A 12-step home group
- An alternative type of support group (for example, grief)
- An accountability partner or group
- A cultural organization
- A nearby sports facility
- A sports league near you
- An organization (such as a library) that offers courses in skills like computer literacy
- Nearby walking and bike trails
- Having access to a canoe, bike, or other recreational equipment
- A nearby health club or martial arts center
- A stable living situation
- A good job
- Adequate pay
- A working plan for a TLC you already have in place

When writing your TLCs in Chapter 4, you can consult the list of strengths and resources in the back of the book to help you identify your own.

In any area of a TLC in which you already do a great job, under Current Status, note what you're doing. Then, for your goals, write something like "I will continue to take the vitamins I currently take, as they are appropriate and nothing more is necessary." Strengths and resources would then say something like "Current success, consistency, a working plan in place."

Now, on to Chapter 3 and detailed instructions for writing your goals!

3

Writing TLCs: Typical First Try, Better, and Best Versions

This section includes concrete examples of how to write different TLC sections. Remember, your goals must be attainable in order for your TLCs to make a substantive difference in your life. Notice how each attempt to be more specific evolves.

Your first try is likely to be too general. The next try will probably be better but still not specific enough. Your third try will likely be the most specific, and therefore, the most attainable.

Here are some sample TLCs with first attempts, better versions, and best versions.

Note: Not every TLC area has been covered in this section, only some major ones to give you an idea of how to write effective goals. Refer back to chapter two for basic examples in the areas not included here.

Spiritual Enhancement: Prayer and Meditation
First try

Current status: I do not pray or meditate.

Projected goal: I will read the Al-Anon meditation book 20 minutes per day and connect with my Higher Power for 10 minutes.

Strengths and resources to accomplish goal: Faith

Better

Current status: I do not pray or meditate.

Projected goal: I will read the Al-Anon meditation book 20 minutes each day in the morning and connect with my Higher Power for 10 minutes after that.

Strengths and resources to accomplish goal: Faith, self-care

Best

Current status: I do not do anything to express my spirituality.

Projected goal: I will read, reflect, and meditate on the daily reading from Al-Anon's meditation book, *Courage to Change,* for 20 minutes per day the first thing in the morning, at 6:30 a.m. I will journal about the most important insights I've gained. When I am finished, I will spend 10 minutes in prayer, gratitude, or just listening to God. I have set up my schedule so I do not have any commitments before 7 a.m. I will talk to my sponsor about my journaling insights once per month and I have noted this on my calendar.

Strengths and resources to accomplish goal: Faith, love of my Higher Power, desire for spiritual health, experienced sponsor, and self-care

Family Relationships

First try

Current status: I want to fly fish but I never plan any outings.

Projected goal: I will watch a video about fly fishing.

Strengths and resources to accomplish goal: Love of nature and the outdoors

Better

Current status: I go fishing with my family every few weeks. I'd love to try fly fishing, but I've never taken the steps needed to make that happen.

Projected goal: I will ask someone to teach me how to fly fish.

Strengths and resources to accomplish goal: Love of nature and the outdoors, family bonds

Best

Current status: I want to learn how to fly fish in conjunction with one of my family fishing trips.

Projected goal: I will schedule Sunday afternoons twice a month to go fishing with my family. In September, I will ask my friend who knows how to fly fish to come with us for three training sessions.

Strengths and resources to accomplish goal: Love of nature, strong family bonds, helpful friend, current success, careful planning

Social Relationships
First try
Current status: I hang out with friends when I can.

Projected goal: I will hang out with friends more often.

Strengths or resources to accomplish goal: Love of people

Better
Current status: I hang out with friends after class when I can.

Projected goal: I will try to hang out with my friends at least twice a week, either after class or by going out.

Strength and resources to accomplish goal: Social skills, extraversion, good friends

Best
Current status: I hang out with friends after class when I can.

Projected goal: I will ask my friends if we can talk after class at least twice a week, on Tuesdays and Thursdays. In addition, I will call or text one of them every week or ask them to come over and work on a school project with me.

Strengths and resources to accomplish goal: Love of people, outgoing personality, friendly, loyal, faithful, having long-term friendships

Support Group Relationships
First try
Current status: I go to AA meetings as often as possible.

Projected goal: Meet more people and become more involved in my support group.

Strengths and resources to accomplish goal: Desire

Better
Current status: I go to AA meetings once a week.

Projected goal: I will become more involved in my AA group by leading meetings occasionally.

Strengths and resources to accomplish goal: Desire, commitment to recovery

Best

Current status: I go to AA meetings weekly and enjoy meeting old friends. I want to meet new people there. I want to chair meetings, sponsor others, and connect with them regularly.

Projected goal: I will go to AA meetings 3 times per week on Tuesday (home group), Wednesday, and Saturday (and more if needed). If new people are attending, I will have a conversation with at least one of them at each meeting. I will check with my sponsor and, if we agree, schedule myself to chair meetings, lead a topic every 6 months, and let the group know I am available to be a sponsor.

Strengths and resources to accomplish goal: Desire, commitment to recovery, love of people, outgoing personality, great home group, other meetings close to home, an experienced, supportive sponsor

Romantic Relationships

First try

Current status: I do not have regular times set up to go on dates with my spouse.

Projected goal: I will designate a time for us to go on dates.

Strengths and resources to accomplish goal: Desire

Better

Current status: I do not have regular times set up to go on dates with my spouse, but I would like to spend more time together so we can deepen our relationship.

Projected goal: I will schedule Friday night to go on dates with my spouse. I will get my spouse to approve this schedule and, if needed, change to a different night.

Strengths and resources to accomplish goal: Desire, love of spouse, fun-loving personality

Best

Current status: I rarely go on dates with my spouse.

Projected goal: I will discuss going on dates with my spouse tonight after the kids are in bed. If my spouse is agreeable, I will schedule time on Thursday nights every other week for us to go out together. I will call the babysitter tomorrow to schedule the nights, which I will put on my calendar.

Strengths and resources to accomplish goal: Love of spouse, fun-loving personality, creativity, organization and planning skills, trustworthy babysitter in my neighborhood

Service to Society
First try

Current status: I have always wanted to volunteer for Habitat for Humanity and my church.

Projected goal: I will take a more active role in my church.

Strengths and resources to accomplish goal: Love of God

Better

Current status: I have always wanted to volunteer for Habitat for Humanity, but I've never called them to find out how to get involved. I attend church, but I am not involved in any church activities or volunteering.

Projected goals: I will become active by ushering at my church. I will call Habitat for Humanity and see how I could get involved.

Strengths and resources to accomplish goal: Love of God, desire to be of service

Best

Current status: I have always wanted to volunteer for Habitat for Humanity, but I have never called to find out how to get involved. I attend church but I am not involved in church activities or volunteering. I would like to make regular volunteering at Habitat and my church a priority.

Projected goals: I will become active in Habitat for Humanity and my church. I will contact Habitat for Humanity today and see when the next build is coming up and how I can volunteer. I will fill out the forms and submit everything by the end of the week. I will contact the church office tomorrow, sign up, and get on the rotation to usher. I have put all of this on my to-do list (and set a reminder on my phone) for the different steps. I will note when I am scheduled for this volunteering on my phone and calendar.

Strengths and resources to accomplish goal: Love of God, desire to be of service, self-discipline, time management and technology skills, active Habitat for Humanity group, wonderful church community near me

Cultural Identity
  First try
  Current status: I used to feel proud of my racial identity, but I have become disconnected from it.
  Projected goal: I want to feel pride about my racial identity.
  Strengths and resources to accomplish goal: Prior success
  Better
  Current status: I used to feel pride in my racial identity, and I want to feel that again.
  Projected goal: I will ask my parents about our family's cultural background and learn more about heroes from our past.
  Strengths and resources to accomplish goal: Prior success, commitment
  Best
  Current status: I used to feel pride in my racial identity, and I want to feel this again. I want to learn more about my people and our history, how oppression has affected us, and how we overcame it.
  Projected goal: I will start making positive statements about my cultural identity daily to myself and others. I will research my family's cultural history by consulting my parents this weekend at Sunday brunch and using genealogical services on the Internet and at the library on Wednesday nights from 7 to 9 p.m. for the next few weeks. I have set a reminder on my phone. Next month, I will research cultural heroes who have inspired me and write a list of their strengths that I can imitate.
  Strengths and resources to accomplish goal: Prior success, commitment, willingness to learn, supportive family, technological skill, library with genealogy department close by, strong cultural organizations

Exercise: Aerobic

First try

Current status: I used to walk three days per week.

Projected goal: I want to start walking again and add trampoline work.

Strengths and resources to accomplish goal: Prior success

Better

Current status: I used to walk three days per week before school started. I want to start walking again and I would like to add work on my trampoline.

Projected goal: I will walk up and down the stairs at school and in my apartment complex two days per week and work out on my trampoline three days per week.

Strengths and resources to accomplish goal: Hard worker, prior success, commitment

Best

Current status: I live in an apartment building without a gym. I was walking 3 days a week until about a month ago, when school started. I want to start walking again and would like to add work on my mini trampoline or swimming when I can get access to a pool.

Projected goal: I will resume exercising. I will get in 20 minutes of exercise on Monday, Wednesday, Friday, and Saturday at 4:00 p.m. by rotating jumping on the trampoline (Monday and Friday), and walking up and down stairs (Wednesday and Saturday). In the summer, on Monday and Friday, I will swim instead of jump on the trampoline. I have set a reminder on my phone and put it on my calendar.

Strengths and resources to achieve goal: Prior success, commitment, hard working, technological aptitude, nearby neighborhood pool

Exercise: Outdoors in Nature

First try

Current status: I do not get outdoors much.

Projected goal: Go on hikes.

Strengths and resources to accomplish goal: Free time

Better

Current status: I do not get outdoors much.

Projected goal: Go on a hike or jog once per week.

Strengths and resources to accomplish goal: Free time on weekends

Best

Current status: I only get outdoors on some weekends right now, and I wish I could do it more.

Projected goal: I will go on a hike or jog on Sunday afternoon at 3 p.m. I will make a list of all the good things that happened in the past week and practice feeling grateful while I am exercising.

Strengths and resources to accomplish goal: Free time on weekends, self-care, desire for health, a nearby park and walking trails

Sleep

First try

Current status: I get about 6 hours of sleep per night.

Projected goal: I want to get more sleep.

Strengths and resources to accomplish goal: Desire

Better

Current status: I get about 6 hours of sleep per night but I need at least 8.

Projected goal: To get more sleep, I will get to bed by 10 p.m. and get up at 6 a.m.

Strengths and resources to accomplish goal: Desire, commitment, technological aptitude

Best

Current status: I get about 6 hours of sleep per night but I need at least 8. I wake up tired and have a hard time getting out of bed. I typically have to set multiple alarms.

Projected goal: I will turn off the TV and other electronic devices by 9 p.m. and get in bed by 10, then wake up at 6 a.m. I will set a reminder on my phone for bedtime, and will only need to set one alarm in the morning. I will get up when the alarm goes off.

Strengths and resources to accomplish goal: Commitment, stable lifestyle

Nutrition

First try

Current status: I try to cook when I can.

Projected goal: I will cook balanced meals for dinner.

Strengths and resources to accomplish goal: Desire for health

Better

Current status: I try to cook when I have time, but I would like to cook balanced meals more often.

Projected goal: I will cook full dinners that include items from all the food groups.

Strengths and resources to accomplish goal: Desire for health, creativity

Best

Current status: I try to cook when I have time, but I want to prepare balanced meals for myself to enhance my health. I like trying new recipes. Cooking would also be something creative for me to do.

Projected goal: I will cook a full meal that includes items from all 4 food groups for dinner on Fridays, Saturdays, and Sundays. After two weeks, I will also make dinner on Tuesdays and Thursdays. On Sunday afternoon, after my walk, I will make a list of meals that I want to cook or look up new recipes to try.

Strengths and resources to accomplish goal: Desire for health, creativity, love of cooking, commitment, organizational skills

Hydration

First try

Current status: I do not drink enough water.

Projected goal: I will drink more water.

Strengths and resources to accomplish goal: Desire, commitment

Better

Current status: I do not make it a priority to drink enough water throughout my day.

Projected goal: I will drink water at meals.

Strengths and resources to accomplish goal: Desire for health, commitment

Best

Current status: I drink two glasses of water a day, but I know I need more. I often feel tired and sometimes I get headaches; perhaps staying well hydrated could help me feel better.

Projected goal: I will increase my water intake to at least four glasses per day as follows: one 16-oz. glass at each meal, 8 oz. after getting up, and 8 oz. before going to bed. When exercising, I will drink at least an additional 8 oz. to refuel. I will keep a checklist by my placemat or record on my phone the number of glasses I've drunk. I will bring my water bottle to work so I can drink water when I get thirsty.

Strengths and resources to accomplish goal: Desire for health, self-care, willingness to try new things, large water bottle

Physical Health

First try

Current status: I do not keep up with healthcare appointments.

Projected goal: I want to make more appointments, especially dental.

Strengths and resources to accomplish goal: Desire

Better

Current status: I do not keep up with medical and dental appointments. I want to be more on top of this.

Projected goal: I will schedule a dental appointment next week.

Strengths and resources to accomplish goal: Desire

Best

Current status: I have not kept up with my medical and dental appointments, but I want to change that.

Projected goal: I will call the dentist's office today and schedule an appointment. When I go, I will schedule another appointment for 6 months out. I will call the doctor's office tomorrow and schedule a physical exam and blood test. I have set reminders on my phone.

Strengths and resources to accomplish goal: Commitment to health, self-discipline, planning skills, technological skills

Mental and Emotional Health

First try

Current status: Anxiety is ongoing.

Projected goal: I want to try to think positive and not worry.

Strengths and resources to accomplish goal: Desire

Better (more specific)

Current status: I get anxious daily, have past trauma, and am considering seeing a therapist.

Projected goal: I will look for and find a good therapist and set up an appointment this week.

Strengths and resources to accomplish goal: Determination

Best

Current status: I realize that I need to see a therapist for anxiety and past-trauma issues.

Projected goal: I will search for a therapist who does cognitive behavioral therapy and EMDR and who accepts my insurance plan. I will schedule an appointment by the end of this week (Friday at 4 p.m.). I will also listen to *Feeling Good: The New Mood Therapy* on my way to and from work each day.

Strengths and resources to accomplish goal: Desire, determination, commitment, planning skills, organizational skills

Work

First try

Current status: I am consistently overworking.

Projected goal: I will try to stop work on time.

Strengths and resources to accomplish goal: Desire

Better

Current status: Consistently overworking is leading to my symptoms of burnout.

Projected goal: I will leave work by 5 p.m. I have set a reminder on my phone.

Strengths and resources to accomplish goal: Desire

Best

Current status: I am not sure what factors are causing me to overwork; I want to investigate that and my symptoms of burnout and develop a comprehensive plan to take care of myself.

Projected goal: I will leave work by 5 p.m. I have set a reminder on my phone. This weekend, I will set aside time on Friday and Saturday afternoons from 1–5 p.m. to journal about work, list my symptoms of burnout, and develop a comprehensive plan. I will include work-related stressors, projects due, and possible remedies for self-care through TLCs and supervisor support. I will set up a schedule to meet all my needs and put all deadlines with reminders on my calendar.

Strengths and resources to accomplish goal: Planning, time management and organizational skills, a new planning calendar

Finances
　First try
　Current status: I spend money impulsively.
　Projected goal: I will watch my spending and start saving.
　Strengths and resources to accomplish goal: Self-control
　Better
　Current status: I spend money impulsively on random things.
　Projected goal: I will think about my purchases before I make them and try to save more.
　Strengths and resources to accomplish goal: Self-control
　Best
　Current status: I spend money impulsively on random things. This happens most often when I shop at the mall, rather than in boutiques.
　Projected goal: I will only go to the mall with friends and will go to boutiques or a local store when I am on my own. I will think carefully before I make my purchases and, if I pass up an item, I will save that money in a fund for the vacation to Europe I've wanted to take.

Brain Work (Higher Education)
　First try
　Current status: Attending college but struggling

Projected goal: Finish college

Strengths and resources to accomplish goal: Desire

Better

Current status: I am attending college to get a degree in human services. I don't always complete my assignments because I haven't planned my time well enough.

Projected goal: Finish college in the spring of [year]. Work on a plan to stay on track.

Strengths and resources to accomplish goal: Desire for success, ability to plan

Best

Current status: I am having some problems handing in assignments on time in some of my college classes. I find it hard to balance all aspects of my life and get everything done.

Projected goal: I will schedule with someone at the student resources center on campus at the beginning of each semester to plan my study schedule, and at the end to help me finish the semester strong. I will also schedule library assistance sessions at the beginning of each semester to receive help on planning a schedule for how to get papers done on time and the resources needed to do so. I have put a reminder on my calendar. I will graduate in the spring of [year] with a human services degree.

Strengths and resources to accomplish goal: Commitment, self-discipline, planning and organizational skills, excellent professors, thoughtful academic advisors

Creativity

First try

Current status: I do not draw or do any form of art. The closet I get to doing art is painting walls in my house.

Projected goal: I will begin to do fine art by learning how to paint with watercolors.

Strengths and resources to accomplish goal: Desire

Better

Current status: I want to do other types of painting besides what I'm doing to decorate my home.

Projected goal: I will look into watercolor painting classes at a local community college or continuing education organization.

Strengths and resources to accomplish goal: Desire, nearby community college

Best

Current status: I do not draw or do any form of art. I've always wanted to learn how to paint landscapes.

Projected goals: I will take a painting class this summer beginning on June 3 at the community college, and then plan to have a "painting party" in July with friends.

Strengths and resources to accomplish goal: Desire, curiosity, creativity, willingness to learn, nearby community college

Self-Discipline with Alcohol

First try

Current status: I do not drink alcohol and do not want to.

Projected goals: I will continue my abstinence.

Strengths and resources to accomplish goal: Commitment

Better

Current status: I do not drink alcohol anymore.

Projected goal: I will continue to abstain from alcohol. I will work my recovery program and attend 3 meetings per week (or more when needed).

Strengths and resources to accomplish goal: Commitment to my recovery

Best

Current status: I have been in recovery for 3 years. I have worked through the 12 steps with my sponsor.

Projected goal: I will continue to maintain abstinence with the help of daily meditation from the *Twenty-Four Hours a Day* book and working the steps, attending meetings 3 times per week, and calling my sponsor at least twice per week on Tuesday and Friday. I will make a relapse prevention plan with my sponsor. I will continue to monitor relapse prevention signs once per week and discuss them with my sponsor and home group.

Strengths and resources to accomplish goal: Commitment to my recovery, prior success, peace and serenity, great sponsor, strong home group

Self-Discipline with Quitting Smoking

First try

Current status: I smoke half a pack a day.

Projected goal: I will quit smoking today.

Strengths and resources to accomplish goal: Commitment to health

Better

Current status: I once quit smoking but then resumed it, and now I smoke half a pack per day.

Projected goal: I will quit smoking today and ensure that I have enough support to stay the course. I will focus on relapse prevention for the times I normally get urges. I will call my sponsor to help with accountability.

Strengths and resources to accomplish goal: Commitment to health, supportive family, accountability

Best

Current status: I had stopped smoking but now I smoke half a pack per day. I deeply desire to quit again and am determined to do everything I can to succeed.

Projected goal: I will quit smoking today. I will throw away all cigarettes and reach out to a support group so I can attend the next meeting. I will make a relapse prevention plan, which I will share with my support group sponsor. For additional accountability, I will call a family member or friend and tell them that I quit.

Strengths and resources to accomplish goal: Commitment to health, supportive family, welcoming support group, experienced sponsor.

Make Your TLCs Relevant

If any of these TLCs would work for you, use them. You can also use them as inspiration to come up with versions that are more appropriate for yourself.

With any TLC, if you are already doing something consistently and feel that you are benefitting from it, you can choose to simply increase, improvise on, or expand the activity. For example:

Current status: For exercise, I walk the dogs 20 minutes per day.

Projected goal: I will increase my exercise by walking the dogs for 50 minutes per day.

Strengths and resources to accomplish goal: Current success (already part of routine), organization and time management skills

4

Creating Your TLCs

Spiritual Enhancement

Study and Reflection

Current status:

Projected goals:

Strengths and resources to accomplish goals:

Prayer or Meditation with Journaling

Current status:

Projected goals:

Strengths and resources to accomplish goals:

Relationships

Family Relationships

Current status:

Projected goals:

Strengths and resources to accomplish goals:

Social Relationships

Current status:

Projected goals:

Strengths and resources to accomplish goals:

Support Group Relationships (for example, with a sponsor)

Current status:

Projected goals:

Strengths and resources to accomplish goals:

Romantic Relationships

Current status:

Projected goals:

Strengths and resources to accomplish goals:

Service

Intentional Acts of Kindness

Current status:

Projected goals:

Strengths and resources to accomplish goals:

Service to Society

Current status:

Projected goals:

Strengths and resources to accomplish goals:

Cultural Identity

Current status:

Projected goals:

Strengths and resources to accomplish goals:

Exercise

Aerobic/Stretching

Current status:

Projected goals:

Strengths and resources to accomplish goals:

Outdoors in Nature

Current Status:

Projected goals:

Strengths and resources to accomplish goals:

Sleep

Current status:

Projected goals:

Strengths and resources to accomplish goals:

Nutrition

Food

Current status:

Projected goals:

Strengths and resources to accomplish goals:

Hydration

Current status:

Projected goals:

Strengths and resources to accomplish goals:

Other Nutrition Goal: _____

Current status:

Projected goals:

Strengths and resources to accomplish goals:

Health

Physical

Current status:

Projected goals:

Strengths and resources to accomplish goals:

Mental and Emotional

Current status:

Projected goals:

Strengths and resources to accomplish goals:

Work/Finances

Current status:

Projected goals:

Strengths and resources to accomplish goals:

Brain Work

Neurobics (Puzzles, Chess, Math)

Current status:

Projected goals:

Strengths and resources to accomplish goals:

Higher Education

Current status:

Projected goals:

Strengths and resources to accomplish goals:

Creativity

Fine Art

Current status:

Projected goals:

Strengths and resources to accomplish goals:

Music

Current status:

Projected goals:

Strengths and resources to accomplish goals:

Reading and Writing

Current status:

Projected goals:

Strengths and resources to accomplish goals:

Other Creativity Goal: _____

Current status:

Projected goals:

Strengths and resources to accomplish goals:

Self-Discipline

Alcohol and Drugs

Current status:

Projected goals:

Strengths and resources to accomplish goals:

Screen Time

Current status:

Projected goals:

Strengths and resources to accomplish goals:

Quitting Smoking

Current status:

Projected goals:

Strengths and resources to accomplish goals:

Other Addictions

Current status:

Projected goals:

Strengths and resources to accomplish goals:

Additional TLCs (Not Listed Above)

Category: _____

Current status:

Projected goals:

Strengths and resources to accomplish goals:

Category: _____

Current status:

Projected goals:

Strengths and resources to accomplish goals:

Category: _____

Current status:

Projected goals:

Strengths and resources to accomplish goals:

5

Implementing Your TLCs with Accountability

One of the biggest challenges to sticking with your goals is not having accountability. Firstly, you need self-accountability, which includes checking in with yourself on how you are working toward and meeting your goals. I encourage you to use all your technological resources to get organized and stay accountable. Calendars, organizers, and planners (on paper and on your phone) all work. Remember, your goals need to be observable and measurable as well as realistic.

Outside accountability is also vital, especially with major TLC areas like alcohol self-discipline. Sharing your TLCs with a family member, friend, sponsor, or accountability partner can be very helpful in keeping you on track. If you have an accountability partner, you can request that they ask how your TLCs are going once a week, and you can do this for them as well.

When working on implementing your TLCs, you may find it extremely helpful to take a moment at a set time or throughout the day to review them. I have constructed a daily TLC checklist (see the back of this workbook) that you can personalize. When you review each day, go over how well you took care of yourself and what stopped you from attaining your goals.

You will begin to notice patterns. For instance, one of my students had trouble getting to sleep at a reasonable time and getting enough rest, night after night. In thinking about the problem, he realized that exercising late in the evening was probably keeping him energized. He decided to exercise earlier and make time for it in his daily schedule. By adjusting the time when he exercised, he got on track with both his exercise and his sleep TLCs. Since then, he's had no trouble getting enough sleep. This illustrates how one simple adjustment may be all it takes to get your life balanced and give your body and brain what they need to function best.

You may also need to revisit your TLCs when a situation in your life changes or you want to set a more advanced goal. Begin by reviewing your TLCs at least once a month and any time you have a transition (such as between semesters) or when you experience a major life change (like getting a new job or moving). By regularly reviewing your goals any time your life situation changes, you can revise and update. Then you should be in good shape to continue to benefit from a structured program of work on your TLCs.

Remember to put reminders on your phone, computer, or calendar, or use any other method that will help you remember.

The important thing is to be regularly reviewing and revising to get the maximum benefit from making TLCs. I use a daily checklist to help me stay on track, and I review how I've done with my TLCs on Saturday night at the end of each week. This way, my goals for self-care and growth are continually in my mind, creating new neural networks of positive, hopeful inspiration.

Instead of New Year's resolutions, revise and expand your TLCs to include a new goal! If you are already succeeding, reach for more depth in the areas you feel would benefit you most.

Congratulate yourself when you succeed, and reward yourself with something related to a particular TLC area. For example, after you've been consistently working out for a while and have gotten in better shape, you could join a sports team. Or if you've stopped drinking, you could plan a family vacation using the money you've saved by abstaining from alcohol. Make a list of potential rewards for each goal and identify which you'll give yourself as you succeed.

In addition to setting up ways to stay accountable on your own, you can have joint accountability review sessions with family members, friends, and support group members who are doing their own TLCs. Getting together to encourage and help each other reach goals, such as on a monthly basis, can be extremely beneficial and rewarding. Your success will give others joy, and theirs will inspire you to work harder at achieving yours. Encouragement is contagious! Plus, if you are having trouble with a particular TLC, someone's suggestion, challenge, or even dare can help you revise and improve.

6

Beginning Again

As you implement your TLCs, if you find it difficult and you fail to achieve everything you want, you are not alone. And you can begin again.

When you've worked on making TLCs a reality for a while and settled into new routines, you may become complacent and start to lapse. Think about how you've added new activities to your schedule and how much work you've done and persistence you've shown. Some things have probably gotten easier and fallen right into place, while other goals may have been more difficult to put into action. Perhaps before setting TLC goals, you lived for years without much positive structure; you were just getting by or your life was filled with chaos. If this was the case, then implementing a series of TLCs may at times feel like a major struggle.

You may have gotten all your TLCs in place, only to have something major happen. When changes occur, you may fall back into old coping mechanisms. Watch for this, and during these times, give yourself an extra helping of nourishing TLCs (such as relaxation and sleep). Instead of beating up on yourself for sliding back, pull out your TLCs, adjust your observations for the current situation, and begin again. Negative self-accusations will not help, but positive planning and action will.

I encourage you to build a team of people to assist you. Trained professionals can help you know what your body and brain can and cannot do. You may also want to seek medical advice before putting any plans into action to make sure you're setting achievable, appropriate goals. Friends and family can help with encouragement when it gets tough.

If you have begun using the techniques outlined in this workbook, you've probably begun to see the positive impact that these TLCs can have on your life. When times are tough and you hear a negative voice saying "I don't have time to…I have too much work…I'll disappoint someone if I don't…," remember how much calmer and happier you feel when you have your life well-ordered and your TLCs in place. Boundaries are so helpful in times like these, when, to fulfill others' expectations, you may let what is best for you go by the wayside. Decide what is healthy for you, examine your choices on how to achieve your goals, and then do the things you need to do.

Your TLCs can help you heal your brain and body. They can help you prevent burnout in all areas of life in a commonsense way and feel fully alive in all that you do. Continue to work at your TLCs, and when you get diverted from your goals, just *begin again*.

Strengths

Strengths are your personal qualities, gifts, talents, and virtues, including past successes. You can sum up your strengths in one or a few words, for instance:

- Ability to forgive
- Ability to form long-lasting friendships
- Ability to learn from mistakes
- Adventurous spirit
- Caring heart
- Commitment
- Common sense
- Confidence
- Consistency
- Creativity
- Curiosity
- Dependability
- Desire
- Desire to maintain health
- Determination
- Diligence
- Enthusiasm
- Flexibility
- Friendliness
- Fun personality
- Generosity
- Giftedness in _____
- Goal-orientation
- Great sense of humor

Great social skills
Habit already formed
Honesty
Hopefulness
Humility
Intelligence
Kindness
Love of _____
Love of art
Love of culture
Love of learning
Love of life
Love of people
Loyalty
Motivation
Natural ability
Natural athleticism
Natural talent
Non-judgmental personality
Open-mindedness
Outgoing personality
Patience
Persistence
Self-control
Self-discipline
Sense of fairness
Sensitivity
Stable personality
Strong faith
Successful now
Successful in the past
Technological aptitude
Temperate (moderate)

STRENGTHS

True friend
Virtue
Willingness to learn

Resources (Support from Outside Yourself)

An athletic facility nearby
   A local organization that offers courses
   An accountability group or partner
   A sports league near you
   A health club near you
   A current success
   Access to sports equipment, such as kayaks
   God or a Higher Power
   A good 12-step home group
   A church community
   A secure job with good pay
   A non-12-step support group (for example, grief group)
   Strong friendships
   Membership at a gym or YMCA
   A skilled spiritual advisor
   A devoted sponsor
   A stable living situation
   Strong family ties
   A supportive partner
   Easily accessible walking, biking, or hiking trails
   Having a plan in place

Daily Checklist of TLCs

Spiritual: study and reflection
   Spiritual: prayer or meditation
   Spiritual: 12-step work
   Interpersonal: family
   Interpersonal: social
   Interpersonal: support group or sponsor
   Interpersonal: romantic
   Service: intentional acts of kindness
   Service: to society
   Cultural identity
   Exercise: aerobic/stretching
   Exercise: outdoors
   Sleep
   Nutrition: food
   Nutrition: hydration
   Health: physical
   Health: mental or emotional
   Work
   Brain work: Neurobics
   Brain work: higher education
   Creativity
   Discipline: screen time
   Discipline: alcohol and other drugs
   Discipline: smoking

Glossary

AA: Alcoholics Anonymous, a 12-step support program for people who have a problem with alcohol.

Al-Anon: A 12-step support program for family members and friends of people who have a problem with alcohol.

Cocaine Anonymous: a 12-step support program for people who have a problem with cocaine as their drug of choice.

CoDA: Co-dependents Anonymous, a 12-step support program for people who want healthy relationships.

Cultural identity: Having a sense of who you are within your culture; claiming the strengths of your culture and those in it who inspire you.

Domestic violence: Violence (physical, verbal, emotional, spiritual, or sexual) within an intimate-partner or familial relationship.

Goals: Specific statements laying out what you will accomplish, by what date, and in what manner. Along with current status and strengths, they form your TLCs.

NAMI: National Association for the Mentally Ill. Offers resources, meetings, informational sessions, and support for people with mental illness and their family members.

Nar-anon: A 12-step support program for family members of people who have a problem with narcotics.

Narcotics Anonymous: A 12-step support program for people who have a problem with any of a variety of different drugs.

Neurobics: Exercises that stimulate the brain, such as word-finding and crossword puzzles.

Neuroplasticity: The brain's ability to change and grow.

Resilience: The ability to courageously bounce back from an adverse or

traumatic event.

Bibliography and Extra Reading

Spiritual Enhancement: Study and Reflection

Reverend Benedict Groeschel. *The Virtue Driven Life.* Our Sunday Visitor, 2006.

Matthew Kelly. *The Rhythm of Life: Living Every Day with Passion and Purpose.* Beacon Publishing, 1999.

Spiritual Enhancement: Prayer and Meditation

AA. *24 Hours a Day.* http://www.alcoholics-anonymous.org

Al-Anon. *Courage to Change.* http://al-anon-alateen.org

The Holy Bible.

Thomas A' Kempis. *The Imitation of Christ.*

Relationships: Family

Matthew Kelly. *The 7 Levels of Intimacy: The Art of Loving and the Joy of Being Loved.* Blue Sparrow, 2015.

Dr. Edward Kubany, et. al. *Healing the Trauma of Domestic Violence: A Workbook for Women.* New Harbinger Publications, Inc., 2004.

Pia Mellody and Lawrence S. Freundlich. *The Intimacy Factor: The Ground Rules for Overcoming the Obstacles to Truth, Respect, and Lasting Love.* Harper One, 2009.

Relationships: Social

Dr. Henry Cloud and Dr. John Townsend. *Boundaries: When to Say Yes, How to Say No to Take Control of Your Life.* Zondervan, 2017.

Dr. Henry Cloud and Dr. John Townsend. *Boundaries Workbook.* Zondervan, 2018.

Stephen R. Covey. *The Seven Habits of Highly Effective People: Powerful Lessons in Personal Change.* Free Press, 2004.

Suellen Fried. *Bullies and Victims: Helping Your Children Through the School-*

yard Battlefield. M. Evans and Company, 1998.

Relationships: Romantic

Patrick Carnes, Debra Laaser, Mark Laaser. *Open Hearts: Renewing Relationships with Recovery, Romance and Reality.* Gentle Path Press, 1999.

Gary Chapman. *The 5 Love Languages: The Secret to Love that Lasts.* Northfield Publishing, 2010.

Service: Acts of Kindness

Reverend Lawrence Lovasik. *The Hidden Power of Kindness: A Practical Handbook for Souls Who Dare to Transform the World One Deed at a Time.* Sophia Press, 1999.

Service: To Society

Habitat for Humanity. www.habitat.org

National Center on Sexual Exploitation. www.ncose.org

National Domestic Violence Hotline. www.thehotline.org 800-799-7233

St. Jude Children's Research Hospital. www.StJude.org

Winseman, Clifton, Liesveld. *Living Your Strengths: Discover Your God-Given Talents and Inspire Your Community.* Gallup Press, 2004.

Cultural Identity

American Intercultural Education. www.aieducation.org

The King Center for Nonviolent Social Change. www.thekingcenter.org

Sleep

Dr. Richard Ferber. *Solve Your Child's Sleep Problems: New, Revised and Expanded Edition.* Fireside, 2006.

Dr. Rafael Pelayo. *How to Sleep: The New Science-Based Solutions for Sleeping Through the Night.* Artisan, 2020.

Dr. Nerina Ramlakhan. *Tired But Wired: How to Overcome Sleep Problems: The Essential Sleep Toolkit.* Souvenir Press, 2010.

Matthew Walker. *Why We Sleep: Unlocking the Power of Sleep and Dreams.* Scribner Publishing, 2018.

Dr. Chris Winter. *The Sleep Solution: Why Your Sleep is Broken and How to Fix It.* Berkley, 2018.

Nutrition: Food

Meme Inge. *The Intuitive Eating Guide to Recovery: Let Go of Toxic Diet Culture,*

Reconnect with Food, and Build Self-Love. Rockridge Press, 2020.

Melaleuca, The Wellness Institute. www.melaleuca.com

Shelly Meltzer and Cecily Fuller. *The Complete Book of Sports Nutrition: A Practical Guide to Eating for Sport.* IMM lifestyle, 2007.

Evelyn Tribole, Elyse Resch. *Intuitive Eating: A Revolutionary Anti-Diet Approach.* St. Martin's Essentials, 2020.

Nutrition: Hydration

F. Batmanghelidj. *Water For Health, For Healing, For Life: You're Not Sick, You're Thirsty!* Warner Books, 2003.

Dana Cohen and Gina Bria. *Quench: Beat Fatigue, Drop Weight and Heal Your Body Through the New Science of Optimal Hydration.* Hatchette Books, 2018.

Health (Physical)

Pete Egoscue with Roger Gittines. *Pain Free: A Revolutionary Method for Stopping Chronic Pain.* Bantam Books, 2000.

Pete Egoscue with Roger Gittines. *Pain Free for Women: The Revolutionary Program for Ending Chronic Pain.* Bantam Books, 2002.

Dr. Vincent Fortanasce, David Gutkind, and Dr. Robert Watkins, III. *End Back and Neck Pain.* Human Kinetics, 2011.

Health (Mental and Emotional)

12 Steps and 12 Traditions of AA. http://www.alcoholics-anonymous.org

Alcoholics Anonymous (The Big Book) http://www.alcoholics-anonymous.org

Cocaine Anonymous (The Big Book) http://www.ca.org

Gamblers Anonymous (The Big Book) www.gamblersanonymous.org

Narcotics Anonymous (The Big Book) http://www.na.org

Sexaholics Anonymous (The Big Book) www.sa.org

Patrick Carnes. *Do not Call It Love: Recovery from Sexual Addiction.* Bantam, 1992.

Patrick Carnes. *Out of the Shadows: Understanding Sexual Addiction.* Hazelden, 2001.

Patrick Carnes. *Facing the Shadow: Starting Sexual and Relationship Recovery.* Gentle Path Press, 2015.

Terence Gorski and Merlene Miller. *Staying Sober: A Guide for Relapse Prevention.* Herald Pub House, 1986.

Terence Gorski. *The Staying Sober Workbook: A Serious Solution for the Problem of Relapse.* Herald Pub House, 1992.

Terence Gorski. *Passages Through Recovery: An Action Plan for Preventing Relapse.* Hazelden Publishing, 1997.

Mary Heineman. *Losing Your Shirt: Recovery for Compulsive Gamblers and their Families*, 2nd edition. Hazelden Publishing, 2010.

Caryl Trotter. *Double Bind: A Guide to Recovery and Relapse Prevention for the Chemically Dependent Sexual Abuse Survivor.* Herald Pub House, 1992.

Family Members of Addicted/Ill Persons

Al-Anon. *How Al-Anon Works: For Families and Friends of Alcoholics* http://www.al-anon-alateen.org

Al-Anon. *12 Steps and 12 Traditions of Al-Anon.* http://www.al-anon-alateen.org

Al-Anon. *Paths to Recovery: Al-Anon's Steps, Traditions, and Concepts* http://www.al-anon-alateen.org

American Foundation for Suicide Prevention. www.afsp.org

Anorexia Nervosa and Related Eating Disorders, Inc. www.anred.com

Melody Beattie. *The New Codependency: Help and Guidance for Today's Generation.* Simon and Schuster, 2009.

Linda Berman and Mary-Ellen Siegel. *Behind the 8-Ball: A Recovery Guide for the Families of Gamblers.* iUniverse, 2012.

Claudia Black. *Repeat After Me: A Workbook for Adult Children Overcoming Dysfunctional Family Systems.* Central Recovery Press, 2018.

Edmund J. Bourne. *The Anxiety and Phobia Workbook.* New Harbinger Publications, Inc. 2010.

David D. Burns, MD. *Feeling Good: The New Mood Therapy.* William Morrow, 1999.

David D. Burns, MD. *The Feeling Good Handbook: The Groundbreaking Program with Powerful New Techniques and Step-by-Step Exercises to Overcome Depression, Conquer Anxiety, and Enjoy Greater Intimacy.* Plume, 2020.

David D. Burns, MD. *Feeling Great: The Revolutionary New Treatment for Depression and Anxiety.* PESI Publishing and Media, 2020.

J. Claiborn and C. Pedrick. *The Habit Change Workbook: How to Break Bad*

Habits and Form Good Ones. 2001. Oakland, CA: New Harbinger Publications.

David Clark and Aaron Beck. *The Anxiety and Worry Workbook: The Cognitive Behavioral Solution.* NY: The Guilford Press, 2012.

Codependents Anonymous https://coda.org

Eating Recovery Centers. www.eatingrecoverycenter.com 1-866-623-4599

Dr. Vincent Fortanasce. *The Anti-Alzheimer's Prescription: The Science-Proven Prevention Plan to Start at Any Age.* Avery, 2009.

Dr. Viktor E. Frankl. *Man's Search for Meaning.* Beacon Press, 2000.

Dr. Viktor E. Frankl. *The Unheard Cry for Meaning.* Simon and Schuster, 1978.

Dr. Viktor E. Frankl. *Yes to Life: In Spite of Everything.* Beacon Press, 2020.

Gam-anon International Service Office, Inc. www.gam-anon.org

Bruce C. Hafen. *The Broken Heart: Applying the Atonement to Life's Experiences.* Deseret, 2008.

S.C. Hayes and Smith. *Get Out of Your Mind and Into Your Life: The New Acceptance and Commitment Therapy.* New Harbinger Publications: Oakland, CA, 2005.

Dr. Edward Hollowell and Dr. John Ratey. *Driven to Distraction.* Anchor, 2011.

Dr. Edward Hollowell and Dr. John Ratey. *Delivered from Distraction.* Bellantine Books, 2005.

Dr. Edward Hollowell and Dr. John Ratey. *Answers to Distraction.* Anchor, 2010.

Barbara A. Kipfer. *14,000 Things to be Happy About.* Workman Publishing, 2014.

Mike Lew. *Victims No Longer: The Classic Guide for Men Recovering from Childhood Sexual Abuse.* (2nd Updated Edition). Harper Perennial, 2004.

Emma McAdam, LMFT. *Rewiring the Anxious Brain—Neuroplasticity.* Therapy Nut, YouTube.

Nar-Anon. *Sharing Experience, Strength, and Hope: Nar-Anon Family Groups' Daily Reader.* www.nar-anon.org

Nar-Anon. *Nar-Anon 36* (Steps 1–12) www.nar-anon.org and www.narateen.org

National Association of Anorexia Nervosa and Associated Disorders. www.healthtouch.com

National Anxiety Foundation. http://lexington-on-line.com/naf.ocd.2.html

Obsessive-Compulsive Foundation, Inc. www.ocfoundation.org

Dr. Demitri Papolos and Janice Papolos. *Overcoming Depression: the Definitive Resource for Patients and Families Who Live with Depression and Manic-Depression.* Harper Perennial, 1997.

Dr. Demitri Papolos and Janice Papolos. *The Bipolar Child (Third Edition): The Definitive and Reassuring Guide to Childhood's Most Misunderstood Disorder.* Harmony, 2007.

Reverend Jacques Philippe. *Searching for and Maintaining Peace: A Small Treatise on Peace of Heart.* St. Pauls, Alba House, 2002.

Reverend Jacques Philippe. *Interior Freedom.* Scepter Publishers, 2010.

Karen Reivich and Andrew Shatte. *The Resilience Factor.* Random House, 2002.

Jenni Schaefer with Thom Rutledge. *Life without Ed: How One Woman Declared Independence from Her Eating Disorder and How You Can Too.* McGraw-Hill Education, 2003.

Glenn R. Schiraldi. *The Post-Traumatic Stress Disorder Sourcebook, Revised and Expanded Second Edition: A Guide to Healing, Recovery, Growth.* McGraw-Hill Education, 2016.

G.R. Schiraldi. *The Self-Esteem Workbook.* New Harbinger Publications, 2001.

Richard Sears. *Cognitive Behavioral Therapy and Mindfulness Toolbox.* PESI Publishing and Media, 2017. www.psych-insights.com/mindfulness

Dr. E. Fuller Torrey. *Surviving Schizophrenia, 7th Edition: A Family Manual.* Harper Perennial, 2019.

Dr. E. Fuller Torrey and Michael B. Knable. *Surviving Manic Depression: A Manual on Bipolar Disorder for Patients, Families, and Providers.* Basic Books, 2009.

Bessel Van der Kolk. *The Body Keeps the Score: Brain, Mind and Body in the Healing of Trauma.* Penguin Books, 2015.

Bessel Van der Kolk. *Workbook for The Body Keeps the Score: Brain, Mind and Body in the Healing of Trauma.* Pocket Books, 2020.

Janet Geringer Woititz. *The Complete ACoA Sourcebook: Adult Children of Alcoholics at Home, at Work and in Love.* Health Communications Inc., 2010.

www.therapistaid.com (free downloadable/printable worksheets for many areas including stress reduction and mindfulness.)

Exercise (Aerobic Exercise)

Arnold Nelson and Jouko Kokkonen. *Stretching Anatomy*. 2007.

Pietra Fitness. Stretch Training Program www.pietrafitness.com

Dr. John Ratey. *Spark: The Revolutionary New Science of Exercise and the Brain.* Little Brown and Company, 2010.

Exercise (Outdoor in Nature)

John Colver and Nicole Nazzaro. *Fit By Nature: The Adventx Twelve-Week Outdoor Fitness Program.* Mountaineers Books, 2011

Dr. John Ratey and Bill Manning. *Go Wild: Free Your Body and Mind from the Afflictions of Civilization.* Little Brown and Company, 2014.

Tina Vindum. *Tina Vindum's Outdoor Fitness: Step Out of the Gym and Into the Best Shape of Your Life.* Falcon Guides, 2009.

Work/Finances

Dave Ramsay. *Dave Ramsay's Complete Guide to Money.* Ramsay Press, 2012.

Brain Work: Neurobics (Chess, Sudoku, Word Finds, Crossword, Logic Puzzles)

Kasparov Chess Foundation. www.kasparovchessfoundation.org

United States Chess Federation (USCF) www.uschess.org

Brain Work: Education/Academic

Mortimer Adler and Charles Van Doren. *How to Read a Book: The Classic Guide to Intelligent Reading.* Touchstone, 1972.

Martin J. Bergee and Kevin M. Weingarten. "Multilevel Models of the Relationship Between Music Achievement and Reading and Math Achievement." *Journal of Research in Music Education*, 2020.

Saundra Yancy McGuire with Stephanie McGuire. *Teach Yourself How to Learn: Strategies You Can Use to Ace Any Course at Any Level.* VA: Stylus, 2015.

Expressing Creativity (Art)

Lois Fichner-Rathus. *Understanding Art* (11th Edition). Cengage Learning Inc, 2017.

Expressing Creativity (Literature)

Mortimer J. Adler, Clifton Fadiman, and Philip W. Goetz, Editors. *Great Books of the Western World* 2nd Edition. Encyclopedia Britannica, 1990.

Robert Maynard Hutchins. *The Great Conversation.* (Great Books of the Western World). Encyclopedia Britannica, 1994.

Expressing Creativity (Writing)

Laura Berquist. *The Harp and the Laurel Wreath.* Ignatius Press, 1999.

Emily Dickinson. Edited by Cristanne Miller. *Emily Dickinson's Poems: As She Preserved Them.* Belknap Press, 2016.

Emily Dickinson. Edited by Ellen Louise Hart and Martha Nell Smith. *Open Me Carefully: Emily Dickinson's Intimate Letters to Susan Huntington Dickinson.* Wesleyan University Press, 1998.

National Federation of State Poetry Societies, Inc. www.nfsps.org

Robert Frost. Edited by Edward Connery Lathem. *The Poetry of Robert Frost: The Collected Poems, Complete and Unabridged.* Holt Paperbacks, Revised Edition, 2002.

Walt Whitman. *The Complete Poems.* Penguin Classics, 2005.

What Do You Think?

Please let me know how this workbook has helped you! Contact me at tlcwellnessinstitute@gmail.com or visit my website: tlcwellnessinstitute.com. For more content about TLCs and lifestyle tips, sign up to my email list: http://eepurl.com/hvaeML I'd also be grateful if you'd leave a review of this workbook on Amazon.com.

I wish you love, peace, and joy.

About the Author

Belinda Terro Mooney, LMSW, LCDC, is a licensed social worker and chemical dependency counselor. She has worked in clinical and program management in inpatient and outpatient chemical dependency programs. For ten years, she owned a business in which she trained other professionals, taught, wrote, and conducted a private practice in clinical work. She then stopped working full time in order to home educate her seven children.

Belinda is currently an adjunct professor of human services at Lone Star College Montgomery and a member of the National Association of Addiction Counselors (NAADAC), from which she is scheduled to receive a certificate of achievement for Wellness and Recovery in the Addiction Professions. She is the author of a nonfiction book and two other workbooks. Pursuing writing in earnest and making her own TLCs is helping her recover from trauma.

Belinda's youngest daughter, Gianna T. Mooney, has used TLCs to gain control of her life and pursue self-fulfillment. She is publishing her debut novel, *Stratotech 027*, under the pen name M.T. Lancet in April 2021.

You can connect with me on:

- http://www.tlcwellnessinstitute.com
- https://www.facebook.com/profile.php?id=100065818209832
- https://www.instagram.com/tlcwellnessinstitute

Subscribe to my newsletter:

- http://eepurl.com/hvaeML

www.ingramcontent.com/pod-product-compliance
Lightning Source LLC
Chambersburg PA
CBHW071503070526
44578CB00001B/421